Consequences of Political Violence

CHRISTOPHER HEWITT
Department of Sociology,
University of Maryland

Dartmouth
Aldershot · Brookfield USA · Hong Kong · Singapore · Sydney

Published by
Dartmouth Publishing Company Limited
Gower House
Croft Road
Aldershot
Hants GU11 3HR
England

Dartmouth Publishing Company
Old Post Road
Brookfield
Vermont 05036
USA

British Library Cataloguing in Publication Data
Hewitt, Christopher
Consequences of Political Violence
I. Title
322.42

Library of Congress Cataloging-in-Publication Data
Hewitt, Christopher.
Consequences of political violence / Christopher Hewitt.
p. cm.
Includes bibliographical references.
ISBN 1-85521-399-0 : £35.00 ($49.95 U.S. : est.)
1. Violence. 2. Terrorism. I. Title.
JC328.6.H48 1993
303.6—dc20

93-22661
CIP

Printed by Athenaeum Press Ltd, Newcastle upon Tyne

ISBN 1 85521 399 0

CONSEQUENCES OF POLITICAL VIOLENCE

In loving memory of my parents

Contents

List of Tables and Figures

Tables

Figures

Acknowledgements

I would like to thank the following organizations and individuals for providing me with survey data and other information: *Allensbach;* Institut fur Demoskopie, Zentral Archiv fur Sozialforschung, Universitat zu Koln; Instituto di studi e richerche Carlo Cattaneo; *Belfast Telegraph; Irish Times;* BBC Northern Ireland; Professor Robert Clark, George Mason University; Professor Richard Rose, University of Strathclyde; Professor Juan Linz, Yale University; Robert Cormack and Professor Edward Moxon-Browne, Queens University of Belfast.

Also the many journalists, politicians and government officials whom I interviewed in 1986-87, who gave me their insights into the effects of political violence. Robert Clark, Conor O'Clery, David Paletz, David Rapaport and Dan Snodderly read parts of the original manuscript and gave me several helpful suggestions. I am also grateful to the University of Maryland, Baltimore County for purchasing the polls of Gallup Uruguay. The research for this article was partially funded by the United States Institute of Peace. The opinions, findings, and conclusions are those of the author and do not necessarily reflect the views of the United States Institute of Peace.

Mrs. Pat Richardson typed many versions of this manuscript with unfailing skill and patience.

The first part of chapter two was previously published in 'The Costs of Terrorism.' *Terrorism: An International Journal* (Fall 1988), Taylor and Francis, Washington, D.C. Portions of chapter four were previously published in 'Terrorism and Public Opinion,' *Terrorism and Political Violence* (Spring 1990), Frank Cass and Company, and *Perspectives on the Media and Terrorism* (edited by David Paletz and Alex Schmid, Sage, 1992). I thank the editors and publishers for their permission to reprint.

1 Introduction

Political violence in western society

This is a study of the consequences of political violence in a selected group of Western democratic societies. Political violence takes three forms; rioting, terrorism and civil war. Riots involve unorganized crowds, and the motives of the rioters are not always clear, although they are certainly not always political. Some riots, for example, are marked by widespread drunkenness, the involvement of criminal elements and indiscriminate looting and property destruction (Banfield, 1974). However, some riots are obviously manifestations of political sentiments (Rude, 1964).

In the case of violence by organized political groups, the purposive nature of the violence is usually obvious, since the groups issue statements and manifestos. Most analyses of political violence distinguish between civil wars and terrorism, according to the number of participants and their tactics. Civil wars involve rival armies who battle for territorial control (e.g. Lebanon). Most terrorist campaigns are carried out by a small number of individuals, and even the largest groups have only a few hundred members. Terrorism is directed against non-combatants as well as military targets, and since it is intended to influence public opinion, its victims are often selected for their symbolic value. The primary significance of political violence lies in its consequences. To its proponents, violence is not an end in itself but a means to achieve certain political and social outcomes. Different goals are sought by

1

different groups. Revolutionary leftists try to radicalize the working class, to provoke government repression, to destabilize the regime, or to destroy its legitimacy. Nationalists, believing their land occupied by foreigners, seek to raise the costs to the occupying power in the hope that public opinion in the metropolitan country will become weary of the struggle. Neofascists attempt to intimidate their enemies or to create social disorder, and thereby justify a rightwing coup.

I focus on violence in Western society for both personal and methodological reasons. As one commentator has pointed out 'Rich countries are at once rich in goods and services and rich in data. Statistical records of less affluent countries are, in contrast, quite weak' (Wilensky, 1975, p. xiii). Many of the questions that I wish to examine - concerning public opinion and the economy, for example - can only be answered if public opinion surveys and accurate statistics are available.

However, limiting the scope of the research in this manner makes it unlikely that the findings can be applied to non-Western societies for two reasons. First, political violence varies between types of societies. Second, the impact of political violence is likely to be very different in different kinds of societies. Cross-national studies (Feierabend and Feierabend, 1966; Gurr, 1968; Hibbs, 1973) show that political violence has been more severe in Third World countries than in the West. In addition, poor communications and the inability of the central government to control outlying areas means that guerilla insurgencies are common. Thus, many Third World countries have been racked by chronic civil wars.

In contemporary Western societies protracted conflicts are rare, and have never reached the stage of civil war. Instead, political violence is limited to rioting and terrorism, which are usually far less deadly. Despite the fact that Western nations as a group are relatively peaceful, there is considerable variation among them, and some have experienced significant violence. Table 1 shows the number of deaths from political violence during the 1968-77 decade. The data are the most recent statistics available in the *World Handbook of Political and Social Indicators* (Taylor and Jodice, 1983).

For most countries this period was marked by unusually widespread social unrest, and in the 1980s the level of violence declined significantly. However, it is likely that in the future

Western societies will again suffer from riots and terrorism. This being so, it would be wise to consider the results of political violence and what can be done to mitigate them. However, very little attention has been given to this topic. As one writer points out: 'We have not thought much about the social and political consequences of the routinization of terror. Social scientists and historians have made exhaustive analyses of everything from the causes of terrorism, to the nature of the terrorist, to the relationship of terrorism to ideology. But what are the consequences of terrorism - unanticipated and otherwise?' (Crenshaw, 1983, p. 39).

Table 1.1
Deaths from Political Violence (1968-77) in Selected Western Countries

	Deaths	Deaths/million
Argentina	4543	168
United Kingdom	1454	26
Uruguay	60	21
Ireland	49	14
Belgium	71	7
Venezuela	61	5
Spain	161	4
Italy	150	3
Greece	33	3
Puerto Rico	7	2
United States	114	1
France	52	1
Germany	51	1
Netherlands	13	1
Austria	4	1
Canada	4	-

*Australia, Iceland, Denmark, Finland, Luxembourg, New Zealand and Switzerland had no deaths from political violence. Canada's rate per million was less than .05.

A recent assessment of the field (Gurr, 1988) concluded that 'such topics as the extent to which terrorist groups gain their objectives through violence, the policy changes that governments make following terrorist incidents, and the effects that violence has on a country's economy, political institutions, and society have barely been touched by researchers'. The information that we have is usually case specific, fragmentary and anecdotal. What I do in this book is to examine the effects of political violence systematically through a study whose scope is both cross-national and longitudinal. Political violence has taken different forms in different countries, and therefore one must examine the experience of several societies in order to understand the range of consequences that can occur. Many effects are neither short-term nor immediate. Instead violence is likely to produce gradual changes in public attitudes, social behavior and the economy. To discover such cumulative effects, and the crucial thresholds at which change occurs, requires a longitudinal analysis of change over time. This research strategy enables us to estimate not only the significance of political violence and how its consequences vary between societies, but also gives us an idea of what factors are associated with each kind of impact. Some findings may seem obvious, but others are counter intuitive and opposed to the conventional wisdom.

The five cases

In selecting the cases for analysis, several criteria were used. First, since it is unlikely that intermittent small-scale violence has any effect, I ignored those countries (such as the Netherlands, Norway or Austria) which had less than 50 persons killed in a continuous series of interrelated incidents. France was excluded under this criterion because most of the violence in that country involved 'sporadic terrorist activity on French soil by foreign based groups' against non-French targets (Lodge, 1981, p. 107).

This left less than a dozen possibilities, equally divided between situations in which violence resulted from ethnic-nationalism and those in which it resulted from revolutionary-leftism. Violence was concentrated in two geographic regions, Western Europe and Latin America. From these I selected five cases: Northern Ireland (1968-86), Spain (1975-86), West Germany (1967-81), Italy (1968-81) and Uruguay (1962-73). The conflicts in Northern Ireland and the Basque region of Spain are the most protracted and deadly examples of ethnic-nationalist violence that can be found in Western Europe. Furthermore, given the small population of both areas the fatality rate is exceptionally high. In Northern Ireland, with one and a half million people, political violence has claimed almost three thousand lives, while the 2.2 million inhabitants of the Basque country have suffered 600 fatalities.

The Tupamaros of Uruguay are generally regarded as one of the most important urban guerrilla groups of modern times, and provide a model for revolutionaries throughout Latin America and Europe.[1] Their innovative and sophisticated tactics were copied by terrorist groups in Italy, Argentina and West Germany.[2] Of all the revolutionary insurgencies in Latin America that of the Tupamaros came closest to seizing power, and their campaign served as a catalyst in destroying what was once regarded as the most advanced democracy on the continent (Porzecanski, 1973, p. xi, Laqueur, 1977, p. 118).

Italy and West Germany were selected for very different reasons. Within Western Europe, Italy is the most important example of political violence resulting from revolutionary (and fascist) groups. On the other hand, Germany experienced only low level violence from both the Marxist left and the neo-Nazi right. However, since political violence provoked the authorities into imposing rigorous security measures and a witchhunt for terrorist sympathizers, Germany is an interesting threshold case for examining the level at which violence begins to have a discernible impact.

Although not truly random, the sample includes examples from Latin America and Europe, and of both nationalist and revolutionary-leftist violence. Good data were available for all five cases.[3] Furthermore a preliminary survey of the literature found that some economic, social or political impact was reported in each society. The periods examined are somewhat arbitrary, although the starting dates are those which are conventionally used.[4] Terrorism in Germany and Italy continued after 1981 but at a much lower level.[5] In Spain and Northern Ireland, 1986-7 was used as a cut-off, because it proved difficult to get many statistics after this date.[6]

All five countries experienced protracted terrorism and numerous riots. Economic decline in Uruguay provoked labor unrest and student demonstrations throughout the 1960s. Protesting the governments austerity program, several workers and students were killed in clashes with the police. The election campaign of 1971 'was accompanied by a level of violence unparalleled since the civil war at the beginning of the century' (Weinstein, 1975, p. 125). Confrontations were reported in the high schools between rightist and leftist students. The Tupamaros were organized in late 1962, but did not carry out any major actions until 1968. Initially they engaged in romantic Robin Hood style exploits - such as hijacking a grocery truck and distributing the food to slum dwellers - as well as kidnapping a score of politicians, businessmen, and foreign diplomats. Eventually they attacked the military and provoked an all-out confrontation, which ended with their destruction, a military takeover and massive repression.

In Germany, student demonstrations in 1967-8 against Vietnam, the Springer publishing house and the Shah's visit ended in violent riots. Subsequently a number of radicals formed the Rote Armee Fraktion (Red Army Faction), which killed and kidnapped several prominent politicians and businessmen. In 1977, their activities reached a peak with three murders and the hijacking of a Lufthansa jet. Thereafter the campaign wound down as police captured most of the terrorists. Although the general public had little sympathy for the RAF, violence broke out when their sympathizers protested what they saw as government repression. (For example there were riots when a terrorist starved himself to death in 1974, and again in 1977, when three of the leaders committed suicide in jail).

The Italian disorders were on a scale without equal in Western Europe. Beginning with the 'hot autumn' of 1968, student protests only started to subside in 1970, and for years afterward, thousands continued to march through the streets and battle the police and gangs of fascists. In Milan alone, demonstrations of 30,000 or 50,000 were common and frequently ended in violence. Unlike other Western societies, the working class joined the student radicals, occupying factories and sabotaging production (Meade, 1990). The Red Brigades and other revolutionary leftist groups emerged in this climate of militancy and unrest. Whereas fascist terrorists bombed public places, revolutionary terrorism was more selective. Business executives, journalists and political activists were assassinated or knee-capped. The 1977 kidnap/murder of Aldo Moro, a Christian democratic leader was their most spectacular exploit. Following the kidnapping of General Dozier, an American NATO commander, in December 1981, a massive police crackdown led to the arrest of hundreds of terrorists in 1982.

In Uruguay, Germany and Italy, the violence was inspired by revolutionary ideology and class issues. In Northern Ireland and Spain, ethnic grievances and nationalist aspirations underlie the violence. Communal rioting between Northern Irish Catholics and

Protestants broke out in 1968. Although this was stopped by the arrival of British troops, within a few months the Catholics were clashing with the Army. This chronic state of confrontation between the security forces and the Catholics has lasted for two decades. More important in terms of loss of life are the terrorist campaigns of both the republican (Catholic) and loyalist (Protestant) groups. The Provisional IRA began its campaign to drive out the British and reunite Ireland in February 1971. Their primary targets have been the security forces, but large numbers of civilians have died as a result of their bombing of shops, offices and other economic targets. Provoked by IRA terrorism, Protestant extremists began assassinating Catholics in 1972, and such sectarian killings have continued intermittently since then.

Basque nationalism was savagely repressed under Franco but a resistance movement gradually developed, and ETA was founded in 1959. The organization split into a number of factions all of which consider themselves to be engaged in a national liberation struggle to establish an independent Basque homeland. Most attacks are against the Spanish security forces and occur within the Basque region, although some have taken place in Madrid. Although ETA terrorism accounts for the great majority of deaths due to political violence, other separatist, revolutionary-leftist and extreme rightist groups have been active in Spain. Furthermore protests and demonstrations within the Basque provinces have resulted in several deaths.

What are the consequences of political violence?

Given the paucity of previous research, it is not surprising that no systematic theory exists as to the effects of political violence. However, a review of the literature found a number of claims as to the consequences of political violence in particular countries. I used these to construct a set of hypotheses.

The consequences of political violence may be either immediate or long term, direct or indirect. Most easily seen are the immediate and direct effects; people killed and property destroyed. These impacts can, in their turn, eventually produce changes in peoples' attitudes and behavior in a variety of contexts: economic, social and political.

The economy will be affected as production is disrupted, tourism falls off, people migrate from violent areas and so on. Social activities will decline if people are afraid to go out. Public administration will be curtailed as terrorists and rioters attack government offices and civil servants. Most importantly the ability of the government to enforce its rule over the population may be affected for two reasons. First, attacks on the security forces make 'normal policing' impossible; if police cannot enter certain areas or if they must take extreme precautions. Second, the population may be so disaffected and alienated from the government that they refuse to cooperate with it. The consequent breakdown in law-and-order might result in an increase in ordinary (non-political) crime.

These economic and social changes, in turn, trigger changes in public opinion. Public order becomes an increasingly important issue; defined as not only a personal problem, but as a problem requiring government action. Public perceptions of the insurgents and their cause are transformed as the cycle of violence continues.

To politicians, public opinion represents a set of demands. Political violence becomes a political issue insofar as it achieves a place on the political agenda. The government responds to the issue by enacting policies. Other politicians take stands on government policies. They support or criticize them and suggest alternatives. At this point there is a feedback process. Public opinion may be changed by the political dialogue. Social behavior alters in response to security force actions and other government policies.

The book attempts to test these hypotheses sequentially. Chapter two discusses the economic costs, both direct and long-term. Chapter three examines the social and administrative consequences, chapter four analyzes public opinion and chapters five and six the political process and the electoral consequences. In the last chapter, I focus on the institutional and policy changes brought about by chronic violence, and evaluate the extent to which those who engaged in violence were successful in realizing their goals. Finally I suggest what lessons can be drawn by policy-makers from the experience of these five cases.

Methodologically the study involved gathering data on political violence, and indicators of the economic, social and political situation, as these changed over time. The data collected were of two kinds; published records and interviews with informed observers/experts. The published records included the following:

chronologies of terrorist campaigns and related events, official statistics on terrorist acts and security force countermeasures, economic statistics on a monthly, quarterly or annual basis, public opinion polls, election statistics, chronologies of terrorist-related political events, including legislation, policy changes, parliamentary debates and statements by politicians. These are discussed in an appendix. A small number of informed observers (government officials, academics and journalists) were interviewed to provide information not covered by the published records, and also qualitative assessments.

Notes

1.   Porzecanski argues that the Tupamaros 'presented a viable alternative to the widely-held doctrine that revolutionary wars and liberation struggles in Latin America and elsewhere were to be fought among the peasants and in the rugged countryside....In so doing, they added a new chapter to the theory of revolution' (1973, p. xi).

2.   In Moss' classic study of urban guerrillas (1972) his chapter on the Tupamaros is titled 'Masters of the Game'. Their tactic of trying and then sentencing their kidnap victims to imprisonment in a 'peoples prison' was copied by the Red Brigades as was their organizational structure of cells, columns and support groups. The Montoneros and ERP of Argentina 'modelled themselves closely on the Tupamaros', and their occupation of the city of Pando inspired a copycat operation by the Montoneros three years later (Moss, 1972, pp. 221-6). 'West German terrorists...freely admitted that they had been influenced by the example of the Tupamaros and learned from their experience'. One group even called themselves the 'Berlin Tupamaros' (Laqueur, 1977, p. 176).

3.   Argentina, Venezuela and Cyprus were excluded because good data were unavailable. In the case of Argentina, the violence statistics are notoriously unreliable with wildly different figures given as to the number killed (Russell, 1974). Furthermore there are almost no public opinion polls because, ironically, the files of Gallup Argentina were destroyed by a terrorist bombing.

4.   ETAs campaign began in 1968, but increased dramatically after the death of Franco in 1975, so I have chosen this latter date for the Spanish case.

5.   In Italy, for example, the number of terrorist acts was only 30 in 1986. In Germany most of the RAF members had been apprehended by the early 1980s, although the RZ (Revolutionary cells) continued to attack US military targets.

6.   1986 is also a convenient political date since it is the date of the Anglo-Irish agreement, and also the date of the elections to the Basque parliament.

2 Economic Consequences of Political Violence

This chapter examines the economic effects, both direct and long-term, of political violence. The direct costs will be discussed under four headings: criminal self-financing, property damage, loss of life and security expenditures. The long term impact, whicih may be more significant, is considered under a separate heading. To allow cross-national comparisons, the figures have been calculated in terms of US dollars at 1987 prices.[1]

Criminal self-financing

Terrorist organizations normally finance themselves, in part, by criminal activities such as robberies, kidnappings, extortion and fraud. Table 2.1 shows the cost to each society of such acts. There are several different sources for these estimates including official statistics, event chronologies and citations in books and newspapers.[2]

The table reveals some rather striking differences between countries, both as to the type of criminal self-financing used and the absolute costs of such activities. In Germany, kidnappings were the most significant source of funds. However, in Northern Ireland no successful kidnappings for ransom are recorded,[3] and in Italy and Uruguay terrorist kidnappings were usually for propaganda purposes not ransom. Although the Tupamaros and the Red Brigades carried out some famous kidnappings, they obtained only a small proportion

11

of their funds in this fashion. In all countries, robberies for money or supplies were common. Again, there is an obvious variation between countries, with much less stolen in Germany than elsewhere. In Uruguay and Germany robberies for weapons and other supplies were as important as robberies for money, but in Spain and Italy, the proportion was much lower.

Table 2.1
Cost of Criminal Self-Financing by Terrorist Groups ($ million)

		Ransoms	Money Robberies	Supply Robberies	Extortion and Fraud	Total
Uruguay	(1962-72)	0.9	32.4	41.2	-	74.5
N. Ireland	(1971-87)	-	55.9*	-	43.0	98.9
Spain	(1975-87)	13.8	49.1	5.9	65.3	131.1
Germany	(1967-81)	22.5	6.2	6.4	-	35.1
Italy	(1969-81)	12.5	50.7	0.2	-	63.4

*Includes Supply Robberies

In both Northern Ireland and the Basque provinces of Spain, terrorists raised large sums through extortion. ETA levies a 'revolutionary tax' on businessmen, while in Northern Ireland, both republican and loyalist terrorists demand protection payments from shops and other small firms. In Northern Ireland, additional sums have been raised by cross-border smuggling and by building site fraud,[4] while in Spain there were attempts (apparently unsuccessful) at currency forgery.

Clearly the sums involved are not trivial. However, to gain perspective terrorism should be seen in relation to normal crime. For example, Italy certainly has a problem with kidnapping. Scores of people have been kidnapped, and the lifestyle of the wealthy has changed abruptly.[5] Yet of those abducted, only 8% were victims of terrorist groups, so that even if terrorism were eliminated, the problem would scarcely be diminished. The same point applies to robberies. Terrorists were responsible for only 0.1% of such crimes in Spain, Italy and Uruguay, and even less (0.04%) in Germany. Even if we consider terrorist robberies as a proportion of the more serious robberies, such as bank or payroll robberies, the figure is still only 0.5% in Italy. Only in Northern Ireland does terrorist crime constitute a significant proportion of total crime. Terrorist robberies make up 42.8% of all robberies and 80% of armed robberies, a reflection both of the intensity of the terrorist campaign and the low level of normal crime in that society.

Certainly, in each country, terrorists were able to raise sufficient funds through criminal activities to support a major campaign. Yet overall there seems to be little relationship between the amount of money raised by criminal activity, the size of the organization and the level of terrorist violence. The Tupamaros and the Red Army Faction apparently had more money than they needed to finance their own campaigns, and subsidized terrorism in other countries.[6] Such discrepancies can be explained in various ways. Much of the money raised by terrorist crime is diverted to personal consumption. The German terrorists were notorious for their luxurious lifestyle with BMWs and expensive stereos,[7] while a high proportion of IRA cash 'is pissed against the walls of West Belfast' (Adams, 1986, p. 182).

Property damage

During political violence, extensive property damage can be caused by explosions and arson. The cost of such damage varies according to the number of bombs and fires which are set, the kinds of targets that are attacked and the efficiency of the attacks. Table 2 shows the number of incidents reported for each country. Since the definition of an attack varies between countries, the precise totals must be somewhat suspect, but the overall ranking is likely to be correct. The table shows that Northern Ireland and Italy suffered far more than either Germany or Uruguay.[8]

Table 2.2
Property Attacks and Estimated Cost

		Number of Attacks	Cost (US $ million)
N. Ireland	(1969-87)	10,352	1,734.5
Italy	(1969-81)	8,119	1,360.4
Spain	(1973-87)	3,182	533.1
Germany	(1967-81)	448	75.0
Uruguay	(1962-72)	349	58.4

The only systematic data on property damage costs come from Northern Ireland where compensation is paid by the Government. According to statistics provided by the Northern Irish Office, the payments for 1969-87 total £490.6 million. In the absence of such statistics for other countries, one simple procedure for estimating the cost of property damage is to assume that an average bomb (or fire) does the same amount of damage in each country and that therefore the amount of damage is proportionate to the number of attacks. Given that the number of explosions and the cost of the resulting damage is known for Northern Ireland, the totals for other countries are easily calculated (see Table 2, column 2).

However, there are also obvious differences between the countries in terms of the amount of damage done. Political targets are often attacked for symbolic reasons, without any serious damage being caused. Similarly, the purpose of attacks on the military is to kill soldiers not to inflict property damage. On the other hand, attacks on factories, shops and other economic targets are deliberately intended to produce the maximum amount of property damage. Table 3 shows the distribution of attacks by target for each country. The second estimation procedure takes into account the fact that the amount of damage varies according to the target attacked. 'Cost by target' statistics were obtained from various sources[9] and then multiplied by the number of attacks on that type of target, for each country. The damage totals produced by this method are also shown.

Table 2.3
Distribution of Target by Category (% and Estimated Cost)

	N. Ireland	Italy	Spain	Germany	Uruguay
Security Forces	13	6	15	13	3
Government	8	4	8	18	-
Utilities	10	-	12	11	3
Business	42	24**	24	25	13
Bars, Cinemas, etc.	12	-	6	2	3
Residential*	6	8	13	10	59
Political	3	24	3	9	1
Vehicles	-	16	10	7	19
Cultural, Social Educational	-	14	9	5	-
Other	5	4	1	1	-
Estimated Cost (US $ million)	1,734.5	464.5	407.9	44.2	43.2

*Often houses of government officials or politicians
**Includes utilities

These totals are fairly similar to those produced by the first method, except for Italy where the figures are considerably lower. The lower Italian total is due to the large proportion of attacks on political symbols, noted by several commentators.[10]

The cost of fatalities and injuries

The most obvious effects of political violence are the deaths and injuries resulting from it. In Table 4 the number of deaths and injuries is shown for each society. The totals include those attributed to both terrorism and rioting as well as actions by the security forces. The statistics on deaths are probably reliable but those for injuries are likely to be affected by how an 'injury' is defined.

Table 2.4
Deaths and Injuries Resulting from Political Violence

		Deaths	Injuries
N. Ireland	(1969-84)	2,558	19,488
Uruguay	(1962-72)	112	182
Germany	(1967-81)	71	1,389
Italy	(1969-81)	386	5,084
Spain	(1968-84)	814	3,136

One way of evaluating the death totals is to compare them to deaths resulting from other causes. Several writers, for example, have noted that deaths from terrorism are usually less than those caused by traffic accidents. A more obvious comparison is with criminal homicides. In Table 5 the yearly average of political killings, criminal homicides and road accidents, expressed as a rate per million population is shown. It is clear that in most countries the risk of becoming a victim of terrorism is considerably less than that from either 'normal homicide' or road accidents. Only in the case of Northern Ireland is political violence a greater danger.

This does not mean that the cost of deaths and injuries from political violence should be ignored. Traffic accidents, for example, are recognized as a heavy burden on the economy with the cost of a fatality estimated at close to $250,000. These values are derived by using the 'human capital' approach.[11] This method estimates the economic value of human life by calculating what an individual's future earnings would have been, and then discounting these according to some conventional rate. To calculate the total cost of deaths from political violence we, therefore, need to know the age, sex and occupation of all those killed as well as the 'earnings curve' (i.e. how income changes over time).

Table 2.5
Risk of Death from Various Causes

(Annual Average per Million People)

	Political Violence	Homicide	Traffic Accidents
N. Ireland	97.6	11.9	179.0
Italy	0.6	33.7	172.3
Spain	1.1	5.0	121.7
Uruguay	3.9	68.5	68.6
Germany	0.1	40.4	251.2

In all countries young males make up a disproportionate number of those killed while women, the elderly and young children are less likely to be victims. This demographic profile reflects the fact that policemen, soldiers, terrorists and rioters are usually young males.

The occupational characteristics of the victims vary significantly between the five cases. This is largely a result of the different strategies used by the different terrorist groups. Nationalist terrorists, such as the IRA and ETA, try to kill large numbers of soldiers and police. The IRA bombing campaign, although not directed at civilians, has taken a heavy toll. Most victims of terrorism in Northern Ireland are ordinary people who happen to be in the wrong place at the wrong time. Revolutionary terrorists, like the Red Brigade, Tupamaros and Baader-Meinhof group are more selective, targeting members of the political and business elite. Right-wing terrorists are the least selective. In Italy, as part of their 'strategy of tension' neo-fascist groups set off bombs in public places, killing scores of people. Loyalist terrorists in Northern Ireland have engaged in indiscriminate sectarian murders. Table 6 presents a profile of terrorist victims, by country.

Using these data, the cost of deaths from political violence was calculated, and also the cost of injuries for each country. Estimating the cost of injuries is very difficult. It is probably that many injuries are not reported, and for those that are reported there is often no indication of their severity. The ratio of injuries to deaths shown in Table 4 varies suspiciously between countries. This variation may result from differences between the campaigns, but is more probably a result of differences in reporting. The figures given for the cost of injuries should be regarded therefore as a minimum figure.[12]

Table 2.6
Characteristics of Those Killed in Political Violence (%)

	Italy	Germany	Spain	Uruguay	N. Ireland
AGE					
0-19	12	16	2	11	22
20-39	52	44	56	52	55
40-64	29	27	39	36	20
65 +	7	13	3	1	3
SEX					
Male	81	80	96	95	92
Female	19	20	4	5	8
OCCUPATION					
Soldiers and Police	23	18	44	38	30
Students	16	4	-	5	-
Blue Collar	15	4	7	4	7
White Collar	15	3	8	-	4
Professional/ Elite	10	13	9	3	-
Not in Paid Employment[a]	18	42	3	36	4
Unknown[b]	3	15	29	4	55

[a] Includes pensioners, housewives, children, criminals and terrorists without occupation
[b] Most are probably ordinary blue and white collar individuals

Table 2.7
Cost of Deaths and Injuries ($ million)

	Deaths	Injuries	Total Costs
N. Ireland	464.2	96.2	560.4
Spain	164.2	41.6	206.2
Italy	71.3	11.1	82.4
Germany	18.2	5.1	23.3
Uruguay	5.0	1.2	6.2

Government security expenditures

One might expect that terrorism would result in increased expenditures on security, both absolutely and relatively. In fact, the pattern is considerably more complex. Table 8 shows government expenditures on security as a percentage of total expenditures in the five countries for the year before the terrorism began and for the year when security expenditures were highest. For Uruguay where the army played a significant role in counter-insurgency, military expenditures are also shown. (The Spanish army was occasionally deployed in counter-terrorist operations, but because this was unusual, one could argue that military expenditures in that country should be excluded).

Table 2.8
Expenditures on Security as Percentage of Budget

		Year Before Terrorism	Maximum Year	
Uruguay	(1968-72)	5.4	7.2	(1971)
Uruguay	(Military)	10.6	12.6	(1971)
N. Ireland	(1968-84)	2.3	12.1	(1976)
Spain	(1975-84)	6.8	8.3	(1977)
Spain	(Military)	14.2	15.4	(1977)
Italy	(1975-81)	5.4	5.1	(1976)
Germany	(1970-80)	5.1	5.6	(1977)

The figures are not strictly comparable between countries since each has its own system of classifying expenditures. However, the statistics do allow comparisons to be made over time within a particular country.

Only in Northern Ireland is there a marked increase in the proportion of the government budget devoted to security. In Uruguay there is a moderate increase while the German budget shows a barely discernible rise. On the other hand, in both Spain and Italy, there is a decline through the period as a whole. In Italy, this decline is part of a trend which has been going on since at least 1965. In Spain, the share of security and defense expenditures is more erratic, increasing during 1973-77 and then declining.

Another measure of the impact of a terrorist campaign is the absolute increase in security expenditures during the period. However, not all increases can be attributed to terrorism, since other factors such as population growth and normal program expansion would also lead to increased costs. To measure the impact of terrorism, we therefore first calculate the trend in government expenditures, adjusting for inflation, for the period prior to the beginning of major terrorist activity.[13] Then we extrapolate this trend through the period of the terrorist campaign. The cost of terrorism is represented by the difference between projected and actual expenditures (see Table 9).

Table 2.9
Increased Government Expenditures on Security

		$ million	As % of GDP
Uruguay	(1968-72)	88.3	1.1
N. Ireland	(1968-84)	6,249.0	72.6
Spain	(1975-84)	4,456.8	2.3
Italy	(1975-81)	-4,477.7	-1.2
Germany	(1970-81)	2,696.7	0.6

All the cases show an increase in security expenditures,[14] and in four the increase is greater than the projected trend. Only in Italy was there a lower annual increase during the terrorist period than before.

Due to Britain's international defense commitments, military expenditures in Northern Ireland cannot be calculated on this basis. The Northern Ireland Office, however, has provided estimates of the extra costs incurred in Northern Ireland and these equal $3,468.1 m at 1987 prices.

Explaining variations in security expenditures between nations is difficult. Northern Ireland which had the highest number of deaths in relation to population, shows the greatest increases in security expenditures whether this is measured in relation to GDP or as a proportion of the budget. Apart from this, however, there is no obvious relationship between the severity of the terrorist threat and the increased security effort. In particular, if this criterion is used, Italy seems to have underreacted and Germany to have overreacted.

Political factors may be important. Possibly governments respond not to the overall amount of violence but rather to attacks directed against themselves and other elites. However, this still leaves the Italian and German cases unexplained. In Italy not only Aldo Moro, but scores of other politicians and businessmen fell victim to leftist terrorism. On the other hand in Germany only a handful of the elite were attacked.[15] In Spain, the decline in security expenditures as a proportion of the budget may be linked with the transition from Franco's authoritarian regime to democracy. Thus popular pressures to dismantle the machinery of repression and restrict police powers would explain the decline in size of the Guardia Civil and Policia Armada. In Italy during the late 1960s and early 1970s the police and intelligence agencies came under considerable criticism due to various scandals involving them.[16] The political climate was thus not sympathetic to increased expenditures, despite rising terrorist violence.

Fiscal considerations appear to be a factor. In Northern Ireland security expenditures could be increased without regard to domestic resources since funding came from the British central government.[17] The German economy was so prosperous that a minor increase in the share going to security produced a large increase in constant dollars. In Uruguay, the economic recession limited the amount that could be spent on security.

The direct costs of political violence: a summary

In Table 10 the total costs of political violence in each of the five countries is computed, and shown in relation to GDP. (In the case of Northern Ireland costs are shown as a percentage of GDP for the UK as a whole).

Two things are readily apparent from the table. First that the costs of political violence vary significantly between countries, both in absolute terms and as a percentage of total GDP. Second that the pattern of costs is very different between the different societies. There is, for example, little relationship between the cost of criminal self-financing and property damage, or between the cost of deaths and injuries and the amount expended on security.

The analysis shows that political violence cannot be dismissed as trivial. It has clearly had important and measurable costs in all the cases that were examined. However, there are certainly more significant problems facing society, if we consider only the loss of life and other direct costs. Ordinary crime and traffic accidents routinely take a higher toll in most societies than terrorism. Disasters such as Zeebrugge or the Spanish cooking oil scandal are comparable in the number killed and injured.[18] The significance of political violence must be seen therefore not in terms of these immediate impacts, but rather in its wider and more long-term consequences. Where violence is significant, it is because of its power to disrupt people's lives and to change political attitudes, not because of its economic costs.

Table 2.10
Total Costs by Country ($ million)

	N. Ireland	Spain	Germany	Italy	Uruguay
Criminal Self-Financing	98.9	134.1	35.1	63.4	74.5
Property Damage	1,734.5	407.9	44.2	464.5	43.2
Deaths and Injuries	560.4	206.2	23.3	82.4	6.2
Increased Security	9,717.1	4,456.8	2,696.7	-	88.3
Total	12,110.9	5,205.0	2,799.3	610.3	212.2
% of GDP	4.9	4.1	0.6	0.3	5.3

Terrorism and the economy: the long-term effects

The long-term effects of political violence are likely to be more significant than the direct short-term costs. Terrorist attacks may disrupt production and raise operating costs. In Spain'repeated attacks on the Iberduero power installations caused so much damage that they led to power cuts in 1982 (and)...paralysis of work on Lemoniz leading to costs of one million pesetas a day' (*Keesings,* 1982, p. 31370).

Declining profits, the difficulties of operating in a violent context and threats to their executives may lead businesses to close down or reduce investments. In Northern Ireland during 1961-73 '300 manufacturing firms were disrupted by violence, and by the end of 1974 800 jobs had been lost in 16 firms which had closed permanently as a result of the troubles' (Darby and Williamson, 1978, p. 2). In the Basque provinces of Spain 'factory after factory closed down after 1975, as hundreds of industrialists...packed up and ran to escape ETA's fund-raising methods: abductions, killings

and a steep "Revolutionary Tax" extracted on threat of death'
(Sterling, 1981, p. 181).

In Italy, the Red Brigades shot dead four and wounded 27 Fiat
executives. A few businesses were brought close to ruin by
sabotage. (Sabotage and arson caused more then $55 million worth
of damage in 1977). A handful of factories were totally
destroyed.[19] However, the Tupamaros avoided attacking industrial
enterprises,[20] and German terrorism - although striking at the
symbols of capitalism - was not directed at economic targets.

Certain sectors of the economy suffer disproportionately.
Indiscriminate terrorism in city centers frightens away shoppers and
tourists. People stop going to cinemas, theaters and restaurants. In
Italy after 'Aldo Moro was kidnapped, hotel operators began to
report a growing number of reservation cancellations by would-be
foreign tourists. Real estate agents acknowledged that it was
becoming increasingly difficult to sell property in Italy, as confidence
in the stability of the nation's economy began to ebb. Social events
were also canceled; such as film festivals in which foreign motion
picture stars refused to come, for fear of being kidnapped' (*Time*, 23
January 1978).

Tourism in particular is highly sensitive to political violence. Given
a choice, tourists are likely to avoid areas perceived as dangerous.
Unlike businessmen, they have no investments to keep them visiting
a country. They can change their travel plans or cancel their
bookings - at worst they lose their deposits.

In several countries, terrorists have directly attacked the tourist
trade. In Uruguay in 1971, the Tupamaros launched a campaign to
scare away foreign tourists by writing threatening letters to regular
visitors (O'Neill, 1980, p. 151). Apparently their efforts were highly
successful.[21] One writer credits the Tupamaros with 'ruining the
important tourist business...in 1971 the number of foreign visitors
dropped from 300,000 to 200,000 and the foreign exchange
revenue from tourism fell over 30%' (Shapiro, 1972, p. 102). A
year later, a Uruguayan travel agent complained 'Damn the
Tupamaros and Damn the Government. No one comes here now
except some Brazilians' (*New York Times*, 15 June 1972).

In Spain in 1979 the Basque terrorist group, ETA pm, waged a
'vacation war', setting off 15 bombs in coastal resorts. Press reports
differ as to the impact. *Newsweek*, (16 July 1979) reported that the
bombing was 'a very effective weapon' and that French tourists in

particular were nervous about travelling in Spain. On the other hand *Macleans,* (16 July 1979) downplayed the effects, and noted that 'none of the Canadian travel agencies was aware of any trouble'. In a somewhat crude way, the gross impacts upon the economy can be analyzed by looking at changes in various economic indicators before and after the beginning of the terrorist campaign. For example, if the economy was growing steadily prior to the violence and then the rate of growth declines, this loss in potential production can be attributed to the violence. Two economic indicators (GDP and tourism) are examined using interrupted time series. In three countries there is a significant decline in the rate of growth of one or both of them (see table 11), but there are no observable effects in Germany or Italy.

Table 2.11
Impact of Terrorism on GDP and Tourism

		GDP Decline	Tourism Decline
Uruguay	(1968-73)	-	-324,000
Germany	(1968-81)	-	-
Italy	(1968-81)	-	-
Spain	(1975-81)	-2.9	-290,000
N. Ireland	(1968-81)	-1.3	-79,000

The GDP decline is calculated as the percentage change in the annual rate of growth for the period after political violence breaks out compared to the period before. Thus Spanish GDP grew at an average annual rate of 6% before 1974 but only 3.1% after that date. In Northern Ireland the change was from 4.4 to 3.1% after 1968. The tourism statistics give the net change in the number of foreign tourists entering the country. In Spain, the number of tourists had been increasing by over 2 million each year up to 1975, while after that date it continued to increase but only by 1,800,000 annually. In Ulster, an annual increase of 52,000 was turned into an annual decline of 27,000.[22] Uruguay shows a similar trend to Northern Ireland.

It is, of course, probable that other factors besides violence had important effects on both the economy in general and tourism in particular - for example, the energy crisis of the early 1970s and the resulting global recession. However, these results seem plausible and consistent with the pattern of political violence in each country. In Germany, Italy and Uruguay, terrorist attacks on economic targets were so rare that it is unlikely there would be any noticeable effects. In Northern Ireland, there is general agreement that political violence has severely damaged the economy (Rowthorn, 1981, Davies and McGurnaghan, 1975, New Ireland Forum, 1983). To a considerable extent this damage has been mitigated by heavy subsidies from the United Kingdom Exchequer.[23] One estimate calculates that in 1970-80 the conflict led to a net loss of 2,400 jobs, which is equal to 4% of the total employed in 1971 (Rowthorn, 1981). The impact of ETA terrorism was concentrated in the Basque provinces, which constitute one of Spain's economic centers with 15% of the nation's energy, one third of its shipyards and two thirds of its steel capacity.[24]

Notes

1. In countries where inflation was very high, such as Uruguay, the choice of one exchange rate over another can produce a noticeable difference. Thus Mayans (1971) robbery figures given in US dollars do not agree with those of Mercader and Vera (1969) which are quoted in pesos, if converted at the official exchange rate.

2. In addition to published materials, other information was provided by the Italian Ministry of the Interior, the PCI (Sezione Problemi dello Stato), the Northern Irish Office, the Royal Ulster Constabulary, the US Consulate (Bilbao, Spain), and various journalists and academics. The problem of missing data was usually dealt with by assuming that the unknown was the same as the known. Thus where the amount stolen in a particular robbery was not known, it was estimated to equal the average for known robberies. Similarly if age, occupation or other victim characteristics were not known, they were assumed to be the same as that for victims of the same type.

3. It is rumored, however, that a ransom of $1 million was paid for Ben Dunne, an Irish businessman kidnapped by the IRA, and that the Associated British Foods Company, after two unsuccessful attempts on their staff paid $3 million to avoid further attacks (Adams, 1986, pp. 202-04).

4. IRA smuggling and tax fraud is described by Adams, 1986, pp. 156-82. The most important source involves the misuse of tax exemption certificates. Large building firms pay subcontractors a lump sum for work and the subcontractors, who hold tax exemption certificates, are supposed to pay the tax when it becomes due. Terrorist groups intimidate the subcontractors into paying them the money which would have been paid as tax. For an account of recent trials which give further details see David McKittrick 'The Business of Terrorism'. *Independent,* (30 December 1986) Colin Brady 'Rival Terrorist Groups Join in Giant Tax Fraud'. *Telegraph,* (13 February 1987). In Spain, ETA began to levy a 'revolutionary tax' in 1976. For the sums involved see *Annual of Power and Conflict* 1978-79, Clark, 1984, pp. 227-9.

5. 'Kidnapping...reached a record total of 76 in 1977. Since 1970, kidnappers have netted $175.5 million in ransom money...

As the kidnapping spread, wealthy Italians hired bodyguards, barricaded themselves behind sophisticated electronic alarms or joined the quiet exodus from Italy to homes in Switzerland and New York City' (*Time,* 23 January 1978).

6. Some of the ransom received by the Baader-Meinhof group from the kidnapping of Palmer, the Viennese industrialist, was sent to the Red Brigades (Sterling, 1981, pp. 84-94).

7. 'They had to have lots of money, not only because revolutions need capital like everything else, but also because they liked to live well...A high standard of living accommodation was always demanded...solid, bourgeois, respectable, expensive, luxurious...and always central heating' (Becker, 1978, pp. 181,189).

8. Porzecanski (1973, p. 47) comments that 'sabotage was used very sparingly' by the Tupamaros in Uruguay.

9. It was assumed that bomb damage is fairly similar to fire damage, so statistics on the cost of fires by type (i.e. house, shop, factory, office, etc), provided by the British Insurance Association and Fire Protection Association, were used.

10. One writer comments that most incidents involved 'demonstrative damages' such as burning a poster or smashing a window, while another distinguishes between attacks on state property, which often resulted in serious property damage, and 'minor damage done to political symbols'. An analysis of Italian terrorism in 1978 classifies only 194 bombings as 'major', which can be compared to the total of 1,862 property attacks given by Galleni, 1981. See also Russell, 1979.

11. Three studies in Washington DC (1965), California (1973) and England (1978) yielded estimates of $229,000, $208,000 and $288,000 respectively at 1984 values. For a good discussion of the human capital method see Stephen Rhoads (1980).

12. Cost per injury figures are taken from a study of traffic accidents, which estimates the cost at $12,150 for 'serious' injuries and $290 for 'slight' injuries.

13. It would be unrealistic to assume that low-level terrorism, such as that by the Uruguayan Tupamaros during the 1962-67 period would have produced any response. Budgetary constraints will cause a further lag.

14. An alternative estimate for Northern Ireland using different procedures is given in the New Ireland Forum, 1983. The Forum study calculates the additional expenditures on security 1969-82 as 2,642 million pounds sterling at 1982 prices. This is equivalent to $4,503 million at 1987 prices and is close to my estimate for the same period of $5,201 million. Landford, in von Beyme (1985, p. 213) notes that as a percentage of total expenditures for public sector employment, internal security costs have been stable at 10% since 1965 in Germany.

15. One writer suggests that whereas German terrorists attacked leading figures, Italian terrorists went for middle-level administrators producing 'a systematic paralysis of the administration and the economy' Encounter, 1978, p. 42.

16. 'In 1964 the head of military intelligence General De Lorenzo, was accused of using his position to establish the opportunity for a coup d'etat'. Later General Miceli, head of SID, was accused of links with the right wing organizations, Ordine Nuovo and Rosa dei Venti (Lodge, 1981, pp. 78-83).

17. In addition to paying the security costs, the UK government compensates terrorist victims and pays for property damage in Northern Ireland.

18. In Spain, poisoned cooking oil claimed 586 lives and left 24,992 seriously impaired. This is almost equal to the sum of those killed and wounded by political violence, throughout the whole period. When the cross-channel ferry between Zeebrugge and England sank in March 1987, 135 people were drowned.

19. See for example, the account of a factory gutted by arson in April 1976, with the resulting layoff of 3,000 workers (New York Times, 9 April 1976).

20. The Tupamaros committed arson against the management offices of Uruguay's General Motors plant and the warehouse of Sudamtex, one of the largest (and mostly U.S.-owned) textile plants in Uruguay. These fires caused damage estimated at over $1 million each; but (supposedly) they did not directly affect - or politically alienate - the workers involved, since the factories themselves were purposely undamaged' (Porcecanski, 1973, p. 47).

21. Another source says that the number of visitors dropped 40% in the first six months (Moss, 1972, p. 213).

22. Clark and O'Cinneide (1981) take the view that tourism in Ulster would have levelled off in the 1970s anyway because of the attractions of Southern European vacations. They believe, however, that tourism would have maintained itself at 1968 levels, and estimate the loss for the 1970-82 period to the tourist industry at just under one billion pounds sterling.

23. The decline in manufacturing jobs was offset to some extent by the growth of the private security business, which employs almost 30,000 persons. One positive result of the IRA bombing campaign, and the massive compensation paid by the British government, has been the urban renewal of the old city centers of Belfast and Derry.

24. Clark (1984, p. 15) discusses the link between economic conditions and violence in the Basque provinces. He argues that economic decline is a result of Spanish regional policy rather than ETA violence.

3 Political Violence and the Public

Terrorism and the elite

For those groups such as politicians, government officials and businessmen, who are typically singled out for attack, terrorism leads to drastic changes in their lifestyle. In Germany, 'every important businessman has at least one bodyguard' (*New Yorker,* 20 March 1978), while in Italy 'journalists are routinely protected by bodyguards. . . politicians, industrialists, sports and entertainment personalities and even middle-level executives are threatened' (*Atlas,* May 1978).[1] Sometimes the elite go into hiding. In Spain, many leftist politicians and trade union leaders virtually disappeared, fearing rightist assassins (*Time,* 2 February 1977). A German business magazine advised executives to keep their movements and whereabouts secret, and urged them to avoid 'solitary walks and talks with strangers' (*New York Times,* 18 September 1977). 'For many prominent Germans, life resembled a state of siege. Parties, theater events and public appearances were canceled' (*Time,* 26 September 1977).

In Uruguay, the Tupamaros bombed the homes of army, police, government and business leaders, and attacked such places as the Montevideo Golf Club and fashionable nightclubs. They boasted that 'the representatives of the existing regime have to turn to living almost an underground life....restricting their movement, being constantly protected by body guards even in their own homes' (Porzecanski, 1973, pp. 46-7).

29

In Northern Ireland, politicians and judges are normally assigned bodyguards, but given the high degree of residential segregation - which makes it difficult for terrorists to launch attacks outside their own areas - their social activities are probably less curtailed than in other countries.[2]

Soldiers and police are not normally targets of political violence while off-duty. However, in Northern Ireland about half of the police who died as a result of terrorism were murdered in their homes, coming out of church, walking with their children and so on (Thompson 1985). In Uruguay, a 'frequently employed tactic was publicly humiliating individual police officers. For instance, several Tupamaros would surround a policeman on the street and force him to give up his gun; or they would 'search' a policeman's home, frightening his family and taking with them his uniform, gun, and ammunition' (Porzecanski, 1973. p. 46). Some police were so intimidated that they refused to wear their uniforms on their way home, as required by regulations.

Disruption and fear: their effect on the life of the public

For ordinary citizens the impact is less dramatic but their lives are still affected by terrorism and rioting.[Violence destroys or disrupts utilities, transport, shopping and entertainment. It also leads to increased security precautions and frightens people, so that they are afraid to go about their daily routines.]

[Utilities and transport systems are a common target for terrorists.] In Northern Ireland, electricity, gas and water services were all hit by bombs. The postal and telephone services suffered greatly from a concerted campaign to knock out provincial telephone exchanges, as well as systematic robberies of Post Office vans and offices. 'The scale of the destruction was quite staggering: up to mid-1975, 172 vehicles had been stolen and destroyed and there had been 26 cases of severe damage to main post offices. Fourteen sub-post offices were destroyed and 25 badly damaged. Of 195 telephone exchanges, 29 were destroyed and 10 very badly damaged. The Post Office logged 125 terrorist or riot attacks on Post Office buildings, 554 armed robberies on post offices and 227 on vehicles' (Darby and Williamson, 1978, p. 24).

Transport services are particularly vulnerable, and terrorists have carried out a number of spectacular attacks on airplanes, airports, railway stations and other transport facilities. In Spain, ETA bombed Madrid Airport and two railway stations in 1979. The 1980 bombing of Bologna Railway Station in Italy by fascist terrorists claimed 80 lives - more than any other incident. In Northern Ireland, the IRA has bombed railway stations, trains, bus depots and taxi stands, while Belfast's Aldergrove airport was attacked several times.

Surprisingly, the effect of terrorist attacks on services has been slight. Only a handful of the attacks on utilities have caused serious disruption. In Northern Ireland, explosions cut off water to Belfast for two days in April 1969, and later when a pumping station was destroyed in 1971, ten thousand homes were without water for a week. In Rome, parts of the city were without electricity for several hours after the Red Brigades blew up a power plant in June 1978, although the impact was limited since the explosion occurred in the early morning hours. In Madrid in 1982, phone service to over half a million customers was cut off when the main telephone exchange was damaged by a bomb. Train service between Belfast and Dublin has been interrupted frequently by hijackings and real and hoax bombs. In 1976 the line was closed 63 times, and in 1989 36 times for a total of 50 days (*Independent,* 7 August 1989). Outside Northern Ireland, however, travel has been disrupted for only short periods of time, with few people directly affected.

More serious breakdowns have resulted from political protests and rioting. In Spain, strikers protesting government policy repeatedly brought the Basque Provinces to a standstill, in December 1974, June 1975, March 1976 and May 1977. In Northern Ireland, in the aftermath of the riots that followed internment no buses ran in West Belfast, and there were no deliveries of milk, bread, or mail. Strikes by Protestant workers had considerable effect. In March 1972 during a two day strike 'electricity supplies were sharply reduced, telephone service was sporadic and postal deliveries were canceled' (*New York Times,* 3 March 1972). In May 1974 the Ulster Workers Council strike paralyzed the province for two weeks. Most industry was forced to close and there were widespread blackouts. At its worst, electric output was thirty percent of normal, and many neighborhoods were without power for most of the day.

The relatively low level of disruption directly caused by terrorism can be explained in two ways. First utilities and transport facilities are 'hard targets' and can be made even more difficult to attack by fairly simple precautions. While it is impossible to guard all possible targets, the more important ones such as power stations can be made more secure. Terrorists can always destroy parts of the distribution system, such as electric pylons, but this will have only a local effect and the damage can be quickly repaired. Second, and probably more important, the terrorists have little to gain from attacking utilities or transport systematically [Occasional disruptions serve a propaganda function for the terrorists, reminding the population of their existence, and suggesting that the government is weak and ineffective.] However, repeated attacks would inconvenience or harm the general public, probably turning them against the terrorists.[3]

More important than the direct effects of terrorism and rioting are the fear and increase in security that they produce. Press accounts show how [dramatically social life and travel can fall off] as a result. In Spain, after three policemen were killed by terrorist gunmen, 'the night time streets of Madrid, usually clogged, were empty, cafes, movie houses and discotheques were abandoned' (*New York Times,* 4 February 1977). Similar effects were reported in Italy and Northern Ireland. 'I no longer go to the movies for fear someone will drop a bomb', said a Roman woman (*New York Times,* 25 April 1979). It was the same in Trentino: 'Everyone stays indoors ...because of fear. The dinner pail of a charwomen on a window sill will set off a bomb scare - everybody is so jumpy'. (*New York Times,* 26 January 1971). In Belfast 'the streets are virtually devoid of shoppers and those who do venture out are edgy and preoccupied, and they don't spend much time window shopping' (*New York Times,* 7 May 1972).

Not surprisingly people tend to avoid travelling through areas of chronic violence. Those parts of Rome where street fighting between rightists and leftists was common were avoided by both Italians and tourists. Pilgrims visiting Rome during the Holy Year 'were advised to keep away from the Piazza Risorgimento because it was a major trouble spot' (*New York Times,* 9 March 1975). Aircraft pilots refused to fly into Belfast's Aldergrove Airport, after Northern Ireland was declared a 'hostile area' by the British Airlines Pilots Association. In Germany, 'a Hamburg businessman with a meeting in Frankfurt will travel all night by train or car to avoid being blown up in an airplane' (*New Yorker,* 20 March 1978).

[Increased security precautions, in response to terrorism, further impede free movement and reduce social activities.] In Northern Ireland, downtown Belfast streets were closed to traffic in an effort to frustrate car bombers, and the Belfast to Lisburn Motorway was closed at night to prevent it being used as a get-away route by sectarian assassins. These measures were adopted in the mid 1970s, and remained in effect until the end of the 1980s. The consequences were predictable.

In Northern Ireland 'the strain of shopping grows overwhelming as half a dozen times in a morning shoppers line up for 10 or 15 minutes to have their packages examined and their stomachs prodded..... Many department stores run a routine bomb check on all shopping bags' (New York Times, 11 January 1975). In Germany 'travelers are stopped and searched in cars, at airports and at railway stations. Police, heavily armed, are seen almost everywhere' (U.S. News, 7 November 1977). While searching for the kidnappers of Schleyer, a German industrialist, police raided bars, clubs and other businesses, driving away customers. Even the owner of a brothel 'griped about a sudden shortage of customers' (Time, 21 November 1977). In the Basque Provinces of Spain, 'since the state of emergency went into effect, the streets of Bilbao...are deserted after midnight except for police patrols' (New York Times, 25 May 1975).

At its most extreme, violence drives people from their homes to safer areas. In Northern Ireland after communal rioting between Protestants and Catholics, 60,000 people moved from mixed areas into increasingly segregated ghettos, in what was described as the largest population movement in Europe since the second World War.[4] Protestant farm families living in the Catholic border areas fled to the safety of the towns. (Newsweek, 19 January 1976). Some left the country altogether.[5] In Northern Ireland there has been an exodus of skilled workers and professionals (New York Times, 12 December 1982). In the Basque region, there was an annual outmigration of about 10,000 ethnic Spaniards throughout the 1980s as well as some flight by professionals and businessmen.

Yet these societies were resilient and able to adapt even to chronic violence. In Northern Ireland during the height of the troubles, greyhound races were held in the Bogside 'undeterred by the occasional bullet' (Time, 31 July 1972). Social activities may decline temporarily, but revive quickly. By 1977, it was reported that 'people are beginning to venture out for night events if they are properly guarded. Greyhound racing has started again and is drawing large crowds...About 25,000 persons turned out for a night soccer game' (*New York Times*, 8 November 1977). Usually, violence appears to have only local effects. During the Falls Road curfew press reports noted that the rest of Belfast was going about its business unaffected, and throughout the troubles, many towns have been undisturbed.[6] Similarly, in Italy, social life appeared normal even during the most violent periods. According to observers restaurants and movies were always crowded. 'Office workers take leisurely espresso breaks at the corner bar, housewives back from the outdoor market stop in the narrow streets for a chat' (*Time*, 1 May 1978, *New York Times*, 25 April 1979).

Measuring the impact of political violence

To what extent does political violence affect the daily life of the public? Two activities that can be easily measured are cinema attendance and the use of public transportation. If ordinary people are afraid to go out, then we should see a significant decline in both activities. Furthermore, we can reasonably assume that any decline is not limited to these activities, but extends to other social activities, such as going to bars or restaurants, which cannot be so readily measured.[7]

Violence is likely to have the greatest effect on the general public when it is indiscriminate. Bombs in public places and sectarian assassinations produce the greatest fear and disruption, because they threaten ordinary people almost at random. On the other hand, attacks targeted against the elite and the security forces will affect social life the least. We calculated the risks posed by political violence in each of the five countries by classifying fatalities into four categories, and expressing the risk that an innocent civilian will be killed as a rate per million population. (The statistics refer to the duration of the violent period in each society, as specified in chapter one).

On this basis, one would anticipate the most significant declines in Northern Ireland but little or no impact in Germany or Uruguay. In Spain and Italy there should be noticeable declines, but less serious than in Northern Ireland. One method of estimating the effect of violence is to extrapolate the trend prior to the outbreak of violence, and then to compare the projected to the actual results. The difference between the expected and the actual can be taken to represent the effects of the violence, assuming that there are no changes in other relevant variables.

Table 3.1.
Victims of Political Violence

	Elite	Security Forces	Selected Civilians	Random Civilians	Rate/m
N. Ireland	20	717	416	1166	757.1
Spain	66	303	110	140	4.0
Italy	28	85	101	172	3.2
Uruguay	10	35	63	4	1.6
Germany	7	13	12	24	0.4

Table 3.2
The Impact of Political Violence on Social Activities

Cinema Attendance	% Decline
Italy	-11.4
Spain	No Decline
Germany	No Decline
Uruguay	No Decline
Railways	
Uruguay	-16.9
Spain	-9.4
Germany	No Decline
Italy	No Decline
N. Ireland	No Decline
Other Mass Transit	
Spain (Metro)	-29.3
Spain (Bus)	-27.8
N. Ireland	-8.9
Uruguay	No Decline
Germany	No Decline

*No statistics could be found for cinema attendance in Northern Ireland, nor for mass transit in Italy.

The results support our expectations only in a very crude way. In

Uruguay and Germany, travel and social life were unaffected, except for railway travel in Uruguay which falls dramatically. This decline is presumably due to the slump in foreign tourism (noted in the previous chapter). Certainly, since the Tupamaros never attacked trains nor any other civilian targets, there seems to be no reason why ordinary people should have been afraid to travel.

In the other countries, the impact is curiously uneven, and does not seem strongly correlated with the degree of risk. Bus travel in Northern Ireland declines less than in Spain and railway travel is unaffected.[8] Cinema attendance declines in Italy, but is unaffected in Spain. However, for railway travel the situation is reversed. It is difficult to understand why we find this pattern, since railway stations and cinemas were attacked in both countries.

Government and administrative control

No government can claim effective control over its citizens unless it can collect revenues from them, and maintain law and order. Both revolutionaries and nationalists try to disrupt public administration, and often use a rhetoric which suggests that they constitute an alternative government. For example, terrorists claim to 'execute' some individuals rather than merely killing them, and both the Tupamaros and the Red Brigades held 'peoples' trials' of public officials they kidnapped. Several victims were held by the Tupamaros for months in their 'people's prisons'. The Tupamaros talked, somewhat pretentiously, of creating a power duality. 'Power duality begins when the guerrillas establish themselves in such a status and power position that they not only represent a real threat to the status quo, but also command loyalty and adherence from significant sectors of the population. This allows the organization to be seen as a parallel government...to function as a shadow government...to legislate, to make policy and to administer justice' (Porzecanski, 1973, p. 17).

Although in all five countries terrorists bombed government buildings and attacked police, judges and other officials, for the most part, public administration was unaffected. Only in Northern Ireland was state authority seriously challenged.[9] Following internment, Catholics withdrew from public office and refused to pay rents and utilities. This civil disobedience campaign, which began in August

1971, lasted for several months. At least 23,000 Roman Catholic households, occupying about 15 per cent of the province's public housing, went on strike. (Civil-rights leaders put the figure at 30,000). The rent strike cost housing authorities about $150,000 a week and arrears totalled more than $ 1.5 million. Eventually the Northern Ireland government resorted to emergency legislation. By making weekly deductions from government benefits - old-age pensions, unemployment benefits, sickness and family allowances - the government attempted to recover the unpaid bills (*New York Times,* 1 January 1972).

In some areas, the IRA operated as a de facto government. 'Free Derry', the solidly Roman Catholic quarter where 33,000 of Londonderry's 56,000 people live, was a state within a state. There were no courts and no policemen, rents and taxes went unpaid, gas and electric bills ignored. Young IRA vigilantes openly patrolled the streets, while a collection of street committees, citizens' groups and tenants' associations organized the collection of garbage and dealt with the sick and elderly (*New York Times,* 27 April 1972).
Petty thieves and vandals were dealt with in a harsh fashion. Several youths who ignored warnings to stop stealing were tarred and feathered or shot in the leg. Such vigilante justice was supported by many of the local population. In one incident when a woman was beaten for using drugs, her father-in-law defended the action, saying 'Someone has to keep law and order in this area' (*Newsweek,* 24 April 1972).

Apart from the Bogside and Free Derry, the IRA successfully challenged government control in parts of West Belfast[10] and the border areas of South Armagh and Fermanagh. According to one report 'Large sections of the Southern part of Ulster are all but controlled by the I.R.A....the British Army appears in force or not at all...helicopters remove garbage from British military posts' (*Newsweek,* 19 June 1976). To what extent has government control been eroded by political violence? One measure is the breakdown of normal policing. Normal policing is not possible if policemen cannot safely patrol an area, without taking military-style precautions. It can be assumed therefore that those areas where soldiers and policemen have been killed in the recent past, are areas where normal policing does not occur. There is a striking variation between societies in the extent of such areas. Within Northern Ireland, there are only a handful of districts where killings of police or soldiers have not occurred. In Germany, on the other hand, only in four towns were police killed. In Table 3, the number of people living in such areas has been calculated and expressed as a percentage of total population. This measure, of course, exaggerates the disruption to normal policing produced by terrorist attacks. It is only in those areas where they are in constant danger that police are unable to maintain law and order. A single killing will probably produce only a short-term effect. Assuming that each police killing in a given area affects normal policing for one year, we can produce a summary score for each area by weighting the area scores, by the percentage of time that police have been killed. The data indicate that normal policing was substantially reduced in Northern Ireland, and to a lesser extent in Spain, Uruguay and Italy.

Table 3.3
Extent of Breakdown in Normal Policing %

		Population in Affected Areas	Population Weighted by Time
N. Ireland	(1966-75)	78.3	43.0
Spain	(1968-83)	53.9	20.3
Uruguay	(1962-72)	46.3	16.8
Italy	(1969-80)	34.0	11.6
Germany	(1969-81)	4.7	0.4

Law and order

It is claimed that ordinary crime increases during periods of political violence, and two reasons are given for this. The simplest explanation sees the increase in crime as a result of the breakdown in policing, discussed in the previous section. Since police resources are diverted to guarding against terrorism or quelling riots, normal policing is neglected. In Italy, 'with the police so busy, an increase in general crime was inevitable' (*Time,* 23 January 1978).

An alternative view, labelled the 'breakdown of the social fabric' by Heskin (1981), sees increasing crime rates as an indicator of a more general social malaise. The political challenge to the government posed by terrorism and rioting creates a mood of alienation - a rejection of all authority and of all social rules.[11] Several researchers have suggested that in Northern Ireland a generation of children is growing up with anti-social attitudes. The Chief Constable of the Royal Ulster Constabulary claimed that 'the general climate of lawlessness brought about by a decade of terrorism has lowered community restraint and personal discipline' (*Annual Report,* 1979).

In Italy, during the seventies, alongside political terrorism, there existed the ideology and practice of 'autoriduttori'. This concept of 'self-reduction' justified shoplifting, forcing ones way into cinemas without paying, leaving restaurants without paying the bill and vandalism as means of protesting an unjust and exploitive social order (*Time,* 28 February 1977).

In order to understand the link between political violence and crime, the trend in homicides and robberies for all five countries was examined. These two crimes were selected because they are serious crimes, whose incidence is likely to be accurately recorded. Less serious crimes, such as theft, are significantly underreported even during peaceful times. In almost all cases, crime does increase during periods of political violence. However, this tells us little about causality since crime rates have increased in most Western societies throughout most of the post-war period. If political violence causes ordinary crime to increase, then the increase should be greater after the onset of political violence than before. Furthermore, the increase in the crime rate should follow political violence, not precede it.

Using these two criteria, it appears that crime trends in Italy and Northern Ireland support the view that widespread political violence leads to a general breakdown of social order.[12] In Uruguay and Germany, the incidence of crime does not increase, but since the level of political violence was so low in both countries, this is not surprising. The activities of the Baader-Meinhof gang or the Tupamaros were unlikely to disrupt the fabric of society. Indeed in both societies, terrorism strengthened law and order sentiments amongst the general public. In Germany this resulted in a mood of public vigilance, and when the authorities appealed for information on suspicious activities, they were deluged with 30,000 calls (*MacLeans,* 20 February 1978). Police efforts to apprehend terrorists in 1977 resulted in the capture of more than a thousand ordinary criminals (*Time,* 21 November 1977). The fact that in both Germany and Uruguay, robberies declined during periods of political violence suggests that low levels of political violence may reduce rather than raise ordinary crime.

The Spanish data are ambiguous. There is an abrupt and puzzling decline in both robberies and personal assaults in 1976 and 1977, but otherwise a steady increase in crime, which precedes the beginning of political violence by at least a decade. Most terrorism in Spain is carried out by ETA, and most Spaniards regard the Basque problem as a somewhat alien issue. Thus any impact of political violence upon crime would be found in the Basque provinces but not elsewhere. Unfortunately the published statistics are not broken down by region, so it is impossible to see whether Basque crime has increased more than in the rest of Spain. However, a survey (REIS, April 1982) found that the region ranked number three in reported cases of criminal victimization, with only Madrid and Barcelona having higher rates.

Table 3.4
The Social Impact of Violence

	Germany	Uruguay	Italy	Spain	N. Ireland
Increased Elite Security	X	X	X	X	X
Normal Policing Affected		X	X	X	X
Utilities and Services Disrupted			X	X	X
Travel and Social Activity Decline			X	X	X
Increase in Crime			X		X
Population Movement				X	X
Dissidents Control Local Areas					X

Table 4 summarizes the social consequences of violence in each of the five countries. It suggests that the effects constitute a scale of increasing severity. At low levels of violence only the social activities of the elite are affected. When violence becomes more widespread, normal policing becomes impossible, utilities and public services are disrupted, and the general public reduces its social activities. At its most severe, political violence leads to a breakdown of social order and an increase in crime, the deterioration of government authority and population movements. The table indicates that political violence was more disruptive in Northern Ireland than in Spain or Italy while in Uruguay and Germany it had only minor effects. Such cross-national differences correspond to variations in the amount and kind of violence that the societies have experienced. The pattern suggests that there are threshold effects. Societies can tolerate a certain level of violence, but when it goes beyond a critical point social life is affected.

Notes

1. Enrico Berlinguer, head of Italy's Communist Party, was driven to and from the party's 'headquarters in central Rome in a specially designed armored limousine. At the Fiat automobile works in Turin senior executives lived under a self-imposed curfew beginning at nine p.m. and never walked or drove alone' (Katz, 1980, p. 121).

2. The degree of residential segregation has increased since the troubles began. In 1978, 75% of Protestants and 61% of Catholics said that all or most of their neighbors were of the same religion. This compares with 68% and 57% in 1968 (Rose, 1971, Moxon-Brown, 1983).

3. The Tupamaros felt that the use of sabotage was not really warranted and that it could prove counterproductive, in that it would give rise to ill feelings among the public' (Porzecanski, 1973, p. 46). Darby and Williamson (1978, p. 28) point out that in Northern Ireland 'withdrawal of services was the most effective anti terrorist device of all....people regard the attacker as the enemy'.

4. Darby and Morris (1974) estimate that about two thirds of the refugees were Catholic. A 1979 survey suggests that by that date 10% of the Northern Irish population had moved their homes to avoid violence, with the rate of forced movement being the same for Catholics and Protestants.

5. In Uruguay between 1963 and 1975, 700,000 persons emigrated and Kaufman (1979, pp. 24-5) suggests that this included 'political opposition elements....fleeing the escalating repression'. However, most of the emigrants did so for economic reasons.

6. See the articles in the *New York Times* on Cookstown, Portstewart and even Belfast (1 April 1972, 16 December 1982, 12 May 1985, 30 October 1988).

7. In a 1977 Italian survey, 42% said they had changed their habits as a result of political violence and crime, with 17% saying they didn't go out at night. Some social activities may increase. According to one account 'limitations on normal social intercourse may have been a factor behind the sudden, and for puritanical Ulster, surprising establishment of a

flourishing massage parlour trade' (Darby and Williamson, 1978, p. 27).

8. Furthermore Northern Ireland Rail officials claim that disruptions have resulted in a substantial loss of passengers (*Independent,* 7 August 1989), although the table shows no such impact.

9. In Italy there was a brief strike by Italian judges to protest the inadequate security protection provided them.

10. Another indication of the breakdown of local government control was the increase in squatting in public housing. Empty houses were allocated to homeless families by local paramilitary groups. By 1975, it was estimated that 5500 houses were illegally occupied.

11. However, this claim ignores that the fact that both the IRA and the loyalist paramilitaries enforce their own brand of social discipline. This accounts for the low use of drugs in both Catholic and Protestant working class areas since drug dealers are beaten up or killed. (ETA also kills drug dealers, but drug usage in the Basque region remains very high).

12. Heskin (1981) argues, however, that changes in indictable crime rates for Northern Ireland, England and the Irish Republic are very similar, and therefore that political violence did not lead to a rise in non-political crimes. The difference between his results and ours may be due to differences in the crimes examined.

4 Political Violence, the Media and Public Opinion

Public opinion can be considered as both a cause and a consequence of political violence. Those who advocate political violence do so because they believe that violence will change public attitudes, and thus alter the political situation. [The familiar concept of 'terrorism as theater' obviously presupposes that the public constitutes an audience for the terrorists, and that acts of terrorism are intended to produce certain responses from them (Jenkins, 1975). However, the public does not constitute a single audience, but rather a number of different audiences. Furthermore there are important differences between terrorist groups in the strategies they use to affect public opinion.[1]]

Constituencies, and enemies: a classification of public opinion audiences

To terrorists,the public contains two significant audiences, their constituency of actual and potential supporters, and their enemies. However, the two types of insurgent terrorists, nationalists and revolutionaries, define their situation differently, have very different strategies, and conceive of the public in different ways.

Nationalists see their land as being occupied and their people oppressed by foreigners; thus, their conceptual map takes the form of an ethnic dichotomy. For the IRA this dichotomy consists of Irish and British, for ETA Basques and Spaniards. Given that both the

44

IRA and ETA profess to be socialists, this ethnocentrism is often muted or disguised. Irish republicans argue that Ulster Protestants are really members of the Irish nation (who mistakenly think of themselves as British). Protestants per se are not the enemy, only those who are agents of British imperialism. ETA defines a Basque as anybody who lives in the region and who thinks of himself as a Basque.[2]

Revolutionary terrorists see society as divided between a ruling class and an exploited class. To orthodox Marxists (like the Red Brigades) the exploited class is the proletariat, but revolutionary terrorists frequently extend the concept to include almost everybody except for the very rich and their agents. The Tupamaros, for example, saw the struggle as one between the 'oligarchy' and the 'Uruguayan people', and considered the latter to include civil servants, bank clerks and students. At the other extreme, some groups inspired by the New Left had such a surrealistic ideology that it is difficult to define their real constituency in any meaningful way. The German Red Army Faction rejected their domestic Working Class as too corrupted by consumerism and claimed to be fighting for the Third World oppressed. According to one German terrorist

The analysis of imperialism tells us that the struggle no longer starts in the metropolis, that it's no longer a matter of the working class, but...what's needed is a vanguard in the metropolis that declares its solidarity with the liberation movements of the Third World. Since it lives in the head of the monster, it can do the greatest damage there. Even if the masses in the European metropolis don't put themselves on the side of the revolution - the working class among us is privileged and takes part in the exploitation of the Third World - the only possibility for those who build the Vanguard here, who take part in the struggle here, is to destroy the infra-structure of imperialism, destroy the apparatus (Rapoport, 1988, p. 44).

The rest of the world - those uninvolved in the struggle because they are neither enemies nor supporters of the terrorists - can be classified as bystanders. Many acts of transnational terrorism are played out before bystanders, and in such cases the terrorists usually try to avoid alienating them. After an attack on a British Army base in West Germany, the IRA hastened to 'assure the

German people that none of our attacks are aimed at them, but solely at the British forces who are oppressing our people' (*Keesings,* 1980, p. 30293). The distinction between bystanders and sympathizers is not always clear. Thus 'world public opinion' is sometimes an important audience for the terrorists who hope to mobilize pressure against their enemies.

In this chapter I describe and attempt to explain public attitudes towards terrorism by analyzing a large number of public opinion polls. The available survey data are unfortunately, but not surprisingly, short of being ideal. On some topics we lack any information at all. If we wish to make comparisons between countries, the questions are rarely asked in the same form. Although we are interested in whether terrorism changes public attitudes, on several matters data exist for only one point in time.

Three topics will be examined: terrorism as a means of attracting public attention, public opinion and nationalist terrorism, public opinion and revolutionary terrorism.[3] First, however, the role of the media in forming public opinion will be discussed.

How the media portrays terrorism

The role played by the media in forming public opinion is problematic. We need to know first how the media presents news about terrorism, and second what other sources of information are available to the public. [How the news is presented depends upon two sets of factors. First, there are technical considerations such as the availability of sources, news formats, time constraints, etc. Second there are the political values of the media controllers and the extent of government censorship. Furthermore, the media are not monolithic, TV coverage is different from newspaper coverage, and newspapers differ in their politics.]

Very few studies have examined systematically how the media portrays terrorism. Paletz, Fozzard, and Ayanian (1982, 1983) carried out a content analysis of how the *New York Times* and American television covered the IRA, Red Brigades and FALN, Altheide (1987) examined British and American coverage of two IRA bombings, and Knight and Dean (1982) looked at Canadian coverage of a terrorist takeover of the Iranian Embassy in London. They found that terrorist motives and goals were largely ignored, that official perspectives were reinforced, and governmental repression legitimized. Paletz, Fozzard, and Ayanian (1983) note, however, that there were 'dramatic differences in the coverage' of the three groups they examined. The IRA position was often 'presented eloquently' by sympathizers, whereas the goals of the Red Brigades were ignored. The FALN was described as a group of 'fanatics' who wanted to make Puerto Rico independent 'whether Puerto Rico likes it or not'. To see whether similar patterns could be found in the cases for which I have public opinion data, I examined published accounts and interviewed a small number of journalists and academics.

In Uruguay during 1968-9, the media publicized the ideas of the Tupamaros by publishing their communiques and by interviewing their leaders. Tupamaro activities were reported sympathetically and helped to create their Robin Hood image. Beginning in late 1969, however, the government imposed strict censorship. The press was forbidden to use words such as 'cell', 'commando', 'terrorist', 'extremist', 'subversive', or 'Tupamaro'. In April 1971, a presidential decree prohibited all news about guerilla activities except that supplied by the government. Newspapers were frequently closed down for 'subversive' stories, but throughout the emergency the press attacked anti-terrorist policies as a denial of civil liberties, and criticized security force abuses. (Porzecanski, 1973, Moss 1972).

The German media, by contrast, were hostile to revolutionary ideology, exaggerated the dangers of terrorism and supported government counter-measures whole-heartedly. 'The picture presented by the media, especially the press was often one of unmitigated hysteria. This impression could be gained by following the detailed reporting and sometimes obsessive editorials of the German newspapers, both popular and quality ones' (Lodge, 1981, p. 42).

In Italy, coverage changed significantly throughout the period. Initially the media

...were slow to take an unambiguous stand against terrorism. The black *stragi* were of course universally condemned. But at the time of the kidnapping of Sossi in 1974, the then still mysterious red brigadiers were widely regarded as proletarian Robin Hoods,.... Attitudes began to change with the assassination of Coco in 1976 and the Robin Hoods became inhuman monsters. During 1976 and 1977 what little was left of press sympathy was destroyed by a series of assaults on journalists,... By 1979 condemnation of terrorism had become virtually unanimous (Lodge, 1988, p. 107).

Weinberg and Eubank (1987, p. 138) point out that

the media repeatedly communicated vivid descriptions and pictures of terrorism's victims. These portrayals included not only accounts of political leaders, Aldo Moro most conspicuously, but of ordinary people who were killed or maimed as the result of terrorist atrocities. There was also an increasing tendency to depict their acts as ones of senseless bestiality devoid of serious political content.

Despite the growing hostility of the mainline media, radical views were advocated in the 'movement press' - *Avanguardia Operaia, Il Manifesto and Lotta Continua.* Such papers were a major channel of communication and an independent outlet for the diffusion of revolutionary ideology (Tarrow, 1989, p. 230).

Cleavages within the media are even more obvious in the case of nationalist terrorism. In Northern Ireland, the *Irish News,* whose readership is 93% Catholic, advocates the nationalist position while the *News-Letter* is read mainly by Protestants (87%) and takes a unionist stance (Rose, 1971, pp. 343-4). The two papers also differ in that the *Irish News* is likely to highlight abuses by the security forces, and the *News-Letter* to claim that they are not doing enough. The *Belfast Telegraph,* TV and radio have a mixed audience, and consequently present a spectrum of political views. [Terrorism is certainly not portrayed as senseless. Indeed there is constant discussion of the terrorists' strategy and motives.]

[Terrorist violence is condemned not only in editorials and commentaries but also in how the news is presented. One Ulster informant commented that 'it has become a ritual - so routinized that it may no longer have any effect on the public. TV will show the scene of the incident, the body covered by a sheet, and interviews with spokesmen from both communities condemning the atrocity. Then a few days later the funerals with pictures of the wife and kids'.] He went on to say that 'the recent Armagh bombing (in which two policemen and a nun were killed) was a perfect opportunity for editorializing to the Catholic community. The police were run of the mill, but it was the first time a nun had been killed. They all played up the fact that the nun's relatives went to the policeman's funeral'. Condemnation of IRA terrorism is not universal, however. *An Phoblacht,* published by Sinn Fein, and distributed in working class Catholic areas will vigorously defend and justify IRA attacks. Its weekly circulation is about 12,000 although at times it has reached 30,000 or more. Perhaps 10-15% of Catholic households read it fairly regularly.

British media coverage of Northern Ireland is examined by Curtis (1984). She argues that the Irish nationalist perspective is ignored, and that there is an almost total reliance upon official sources, with the result that the IRA is often blamed for killings it didn't do. The British army is shown in a highly favorable light.

> Soldiers were photographed chatting up children, doing their bit in Santa Claus outfits, and, as in one picture published in London's *Evening News* in 1972, accepting a cup of tea in "a friendly Protestant neighbourhood". The army appeared as almost above the fray - brave, tormented, but largely inactive except as a rather superior kind of Boy Scout Troop. There were several stories of soldiers coming to the aid of the local population on foot, in boats or in helicopters.

She details numerous cases in which allegations of army brutality or torture of internees were ignored or censored by editors and the BBC. 'The media worked in tandem with the army's public relations staff' (1984, p. 83).

In the Basque provinces the situation is very similar to that found in Ulster. Since freedom of the press was guaranteed in 1978, the local media have reflected the main political tendencies in the region. *El Correo Espanol* (read by ethnic Spaniards) is anti ETA and opposed to Basque autonomy and independence. During the 1979 election campaign, the paper 'published front-page stories everyday detailing acts of terrorism and violence in the region and elsewhere. Reports on strikes and terrorism filled more than half the news columns in the issues published during the months before the elections' (Penniman, 1985, p. 270). *El Diario Vasco and Deia* (linked to the PNV) advocate a moderate version of Basque nationalism, and tend to be critical of both ETA terrorism and

Spanish security policies. *Egin* is militantly nationalist, justifies and supports ETA terrorism, and is hostile to the security forces. There is a rough correspondence between the readership of these papers and the vote for each political tendency.

The Spanish Press, outside the Basque provinces, portrays ETA violence as reprehensible, as do the state-controlled radio and television networks. Terrorism receives extensive coverage. For example, 'all newspapers and magazines stressed terrorism as an issue in the 1979 campaign. Several papers seized on the problem of terrorism as a reason to criticize the government, parliamentary democracy, the political parties, and even as a basis for defending the need for a military coup' (Penniman, 1985, p. 263). On the other hand, many left wing and liberal newspapers claimed that terrorist groups described by the government as 'extreme leftists' were, in fact, connected to the extreme right or the police (Penniman, 1985, pp. 263, 269-70). The most widely read and influential paper, *El Pais* takes a strong civil liberties stance, and is often critical of government repression.

Although there is considerable variation in how terrorism is portrayed by the media, certain patterns can be discerned.

1. Terrorism usually receives extensive media coverage with the results of terrorist violence depicted in gruesome detail on TV screens and in newspaper photos - dead bodies, funerals, grieving relatives and physical destruction. This phenomenon is presumably related to the media's appetite for dramatic visual images. (Paletz, Fozzard, and Ayanian, 1983, p. 160). This negative view of terrorist violence is reinforced by editorials and interviews with community leaders condemning violence. Justifications of violence are exceptional, and only to be found in newspapers such as *Egin* and *An Phoblacht* which are linked to terrorist groups. In both Uruguay and Italy, an initial tendency to romanticize terrorist exploits ceased once the campaigns became more deadly.

2. The tendency in the U.S., Canada and Great Britain for the media to ignore the social causes of terrorism and its goals and objectives is not found in the other cases. Where terrorism is carried out by indigenous groups their political goals are noted and often analyzed in detail. The extent to which their cause is sympathetically portrayed will depend upon the political situation in each society. In West Germany where revolutionary attitudes are uncommon, the ideology of the RAF was presented unfavorably. In

Italy and Uruguay, however, where Marxism was a significant ideology, at both mass and elite levels, the leftwing media was, at least initially, sympathetic. The editor of *Il Manifesto,* for example, remarked that 'reading the BR's communiques was like turning the pages of an old family photograph album' (Lodge, 1988, p. 106). The goals of nationalist terrorist groups are strongly supported by their ethnic communities and by the ethnic media.

3. Neither do the media invariably reflect the official perspective. In explaining why the U.S. media emphasize government positions, Paletz et al. are probably correct. 'The authorities arrive first and are there to provide details, explanations and their interpretations to the press' (1983, p. 158).   However, in other societies important sections of the press are skeptical of government explanations and critical of government policies. This adversarial stance seems to be a product of political ideology and historical circumstances. The Irish Catholic and Basque press are normally hostile to the government perspective. In Spain many influential publications such as *El Pais* or *Cambio* emerged during the transition to democracy, and see their role, therefore, as advocates of civil liberties against government repression (Giner, 1983, Sanchez-Gijon, 1987). In Italy and Uruguay, partisan politics explain such anti-government sentiments. Many leftist Italian newspapers accused the secret police of fomenting terrorism to justify a rightist coup, and until the mid 'seventies were strongly opposed to the security measures which were imposed (Silj, 1979, Weinberg and Eubank 1987). The peculiarities of the Uraguayan electoral system meant that President Pacheco was elected with only a minority of votes. Thus, not only the left wing press, but many bourgeois newspapers took a critical stance towards the repressive policies he adopted.

Terrorism and public concern

One purpose of terrorism is to draw attention to some cause or grievance. Schmid and DeGraf, (1982, pp. 215-6) go so far as to claim that 'the genesis of contemporary insurgent terrorism.... (can be seen) primarily as the outgrowth of minority strategies to get into the news'. The argument is plausible in several cases; however such public attention is usually short-lived and the political results fall short of what the terrorists want. Violence forced the Northern

Ireland issue to the attention of the British public for a brief period in 1971-72, but thereafter public interest almost disappeared. Similarly within Spain, the issue of regional autonomy was seen as one of the most important issues by 7% in 1978 (Esteban, 1979), but after 1980 is never cited by more than 1% of the population.

Insofar as terrorists seek to attract attention, they target the enemy public or the uncommitted bystanders. Most terrorist campaigns take place in societies where the issue for which the terrorists are fighting is well known. Such issues as Irish unity or Basque independence do not require terrorism to publicize them. Similarly the revolutionary Marxism of the Red Brigades has been a theme of Italian politics for decades.

Usually it is the terrorist violence itself that becomes the issue for the public, rather than the terrorist's cause. One standard survey question asks what is the most important problem facing the country. In Table 1 the percentage selecting terrorism or a related topic is shown.

Table 4.1
Terrorism as a Problem

		Most Important Problem	(%)	Deaths from Terrorism
Northern Ireland	(1982)	Terrorism	34	2,269
Spain	(1979-82)	Terrorism/Public Order	22	455
Italy	(1972-79)	Public Order	16	227
Great Britain	(1971-72)	Northern Ireland	13	155
Germany	(1976)	Public Order	8	25
Uruguay	(1968-69)	Disorder/subversion	4	14

Sources: BBC (1982)
Revista Espanola de Investigaciones Sociologicas (1979-82)
Fabris (1977)
Rose, McAllister and Mair (1978)
Cerny (1978)
Indice Gallup de Opinion Publica (1968-9)

The answers are obviously affected by the list of topics suggested and by the wording of the topic. Insofar as the question forces a single choice on respondents, it does not take account of those who see terrorism as a significant but not the most important problem. In Spain, if we include those who selected terrorism as the second most important problem, the number is much higher. Furthermore, for certain groups terrorism may be more important. In Northern Ireland, Protestants were more likely than Catholics to see terrorism as the most serious issue (41% and 24%). The simplest explanation for the degree of public concern is that it is directly linked to the amount of terrorism; the more terrorism the more concern. This interpretation is supported by two pieces of evidence. First in a crude way, cross-national differences in the proportion saying that terrorism is the most important problem do correspond to variations in the level of terrorism. If we consider terrorism-related deaths, for the period prior to when the polls were taken, the rank order is generally correct. Northern Ireland has the most deaths followed by Spain and then Italy with Uruguay and Germany having far fewer, and this corresponds to the concern expressed.

Second, within Spain, the changing level of concern is closely linked to the monthly death totals. Indeed, it is striking how quickly public attitudes change in respect to short-term fluctuations in the numbers killed (see figure 1). Unfortunately, in none of the other countries are there a sufficient number of observations to examine changes over time.

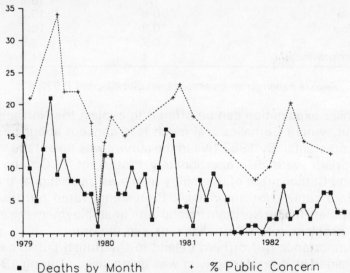

● Deaths by Month   + % Public Concern

Figure 4.1 Terrorism and the Level of Public Concern in Spain (1979-82)

Source: *Revista Espanola de Investigaciones Sociologicas*

Clearly, however, the amount of violence is not the only factor operating on public opinion. In the case of Spain, we can also examine regional differences to see whether there is more concern where terrorist violence is highest. Contrary to expectations, it is those areas with the highest levels of violence, which are the least likely to see terrorism as a significant problem. This can be explained by considering the role of ethnicity in Barcelona and the Basque provinces, where most violence has taken place. Basques and Catalans have strong regional and ethnic identities and sizeable minorities support separatist parties.[4] Terrorism is directed primarily not against fellow ethnics but against the Guardia Civil who are - as a deliberate policy - drawn from other regions of Spain.[5]

Table 4.2
Public Concern in Spain Over Terrorism by Province and Death Rate

	Terrorist Killings/ million Population	Terrorism Main Problem
Basque Provinces	191.9	10.5
Madrid	18.1	14.2
Barcelona	7.0	10.1
Galicia	1.8	16.5
Catalonia	0.8	15.7
Andalucia	0.8	18.4
Canaries	0.7	19.9
All other provinces	1.4	21.9

Sources: *Revista Espanola de Investigaciones Sociologicas* (1979-82)

A similar explanation can be offered to explain the Northern Irish situation, where Catholics feel much less concern about terrorism than Protestants. By 1982 (when the survey was taken) the victims of terrorism were disproportionately Protestant.[6] On the other hand, the Catholic rate of unemployment was much higher than the Protestant rate. Not surprisingly Protestants rated terrorism the main problem facing Northern Ireland with unemployment the second ranked problem, while Catholics reversed the order.

The importance of Northern Ireland to the British public can also be explained by considering who was being killed. During 1971-72 British concern reached a peak, with 13% on average saying it was the most important problem for the country. The salience of the Northern Ireland issue was lower than would have been predicted given the total number of deaths during the period (679). However, if we focus on the number of British soldiers and English civilians killed (155), the concern expressed is at about the expected level. Since the early 1970s British interest in Northern Ireland has diminished considerably, paralleling the decline in the number of British soldiers killed.

Only IRA violence within England now arouses English concern. 'In December, 1974, 23 per cent of respondents thought Ulster the first or second most important problem...The question was asked shortly after an IRA bombing in Birmingham cost 24 lives' (Rose, McAllister, and Mair 1978, p. 26). A similar response followed the bombing of Harrods department store which killed 6 and injured 94. The next month (January 1983) 14 percent thought Northern Ireland was an important problem.

Public opinion and nationalist violence

Nationalists see their land as occupied by foreigners. These foreign imperialists and settlers are the enemy who must be driven out. Their basic strategy is to raise the costs to the enemy until they withdraw. One ETA leader argued that 'nationalistic struggles always try to make the price of loss of life unacceptably high so the enemy will give up its oppression. There comes a time when a nation says "Too much - we have to leave"' (Segaller, 1986, p. 97).

Following an IRA attack in England, the organization issued a statement that said, 'We have a message for the British Government who rule our country against the will of the Irish people. While your soldiers occupy Ireland, we are prepared to extract from you both in England and Ireland and beyond a cost which in the end will prove too expensive' (Keesings, 1981, p. 30867).

These costs can be economic. In Northern Ireland the IRA bombing campaign was intended to increase the financial burden to the British government, who paid compensation to the victims. The purpose of ETA's 'vacation war' was to damage the Spanish tourist industry. The usual way of raising the costs, however, is to kill members of the security forces. Soldiers and police are easy targets, they symbolize foreign domination and their deaths, it is assumed, will lead the enemy public to favor withdrawal. The IRA believed that history showed the validity of this logic.

According to Maguire (1973, p. 75) the original aim of the IRA was to kill thirty six British soldiers - the same number who died in Aden. The target was reached in early November 1971. But this, the Army Council felt, was not enough: I remember Dave, amongst others, saying: "We've got to get eighty". Once eighty had been killed, the pressure on the British to negotiate would be immense. I remember the feeling of satisfaction we had at hearing another one had died. As it happened, the total killed by the time of the truce in June 1972 was 102.

As a strategy for breaking the will of the enemy, nationalist terrorism has had mixed results. The IRA's campaign has been greatly successful in affecting public opinion in Great Britain. Since 1974, the proportion favoring troop withdrawal has remained stable, with a clear majority favoring withdrawal, and a plurality a United Ireland.[7] The metropolitan Spaniards have been far more resistant and the most recent poll reveals that only 14% favor giving in to terrorist demands, or negotiating with the terrorists.[8] The greater resolve of the Spaniards compared to the British is explained perhaps by the relative salience of the issue. If the Spaniards conceded independence to the Basques, other separatist movements would be strengthened, leading to the disintegration of the Spanish state.

As regards their constituency, nationalist terrorists must maintain a high level of at least passive support in order to run an effective campaign. Support can be defined in several ways, as agreement with nationalist goals, as having a positive image of the terrorists and as approval of political violence.

The people of Northern Ireland have been asked repeatedly for their views on 'the best solution to the Northern Irish problem' or their 'long-term constitutional preference', etc. Despite the fact that the options and the form of the question varies somewhat between the different polls, the answers can be compared over time. (Only a handful or respondents refuse to answer or have no opinion). There is no sign that attitudes to Irish unity have changed within either the Catholic or Protestant community since the troubles began. Among Catholics, a united Ireland is usually favored by a plurality but not a majority, and there is no clear trend in the level of support. (The low point in nationalist sentiment coincides with the attempt at 'power sharing' during 1973-4). Of equal significance is the fact that Protestants show no sign of accepting the desirability of Irish unity, and continue to support the British connection.

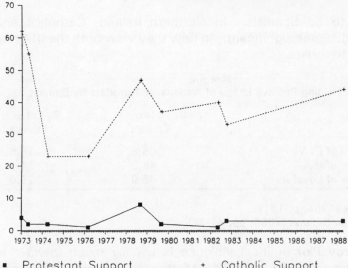

• Protestant Support   + Catholic Support

Figure 4.2 Support for Irish Unity in Northern Ireland by Religion

Sources: Data from "What Ulster Thinks" (1973), Carrick James Market Research (n.d.), "Seven Out of Ten" (1974), Moxon-Browne (1981), "What the People of Ulster Think" (1970), "Public Reaction in N. Ireland" (1982), *Fortnight* (July-August 1982), BBC Market observation Research Institute (1984), and a June 5, 1974, public opinion poll provided to the author by the Opinion Research Center.

For the Basque provinces, Clark (1984, pp. 168-78) presents data from a large number of surveys on support for Basque independence. Unfortunately, as he notes, many respondents 'simply refuse to answer questions about ETA, terrorism or politics in general'. There is no clear trend in the proportion that wanted full independence, although the proportion seems to have declined after the granting of autonomy in 1979.

Public perceptions of the ETA and the IRA are very positive. In the Basque provinces, surveys have asked whether ETA terrorists are patriots, idealists, madmen, criminals or individuals manipulated by outside forces. In Northern Ireland, respondents were asked whether they agreed or disagreed that the IRA were 'basically patriots and idealists'. Both groups are regarded very sympathetically by their fellow ethnics. In the Basque provinces, those who consider themselves as Basque are much more likely to see ETA as patriots and idealists than those who consider themselves to be Spanish. In Northern Ireland, Catholics and Protestants disagree significantly in how they view both the IRA and the Loyalist terrorists.

Table 4.3
Percentage Holding Positive Image of Nationalist Terrorists by Ethnicity

	By Fellow Ethnics	By Other Ethnics
Positive Image of ETA	65.9	15.5
Positive Image of IRA	46.3	34.7
Positive Image of Loyalists	43.9	25.0

Sources: Clark (1984, p. 181)
Moxon-Browne (1986, pp. 41-72)

Explicit approval of political violence is usually much lower. In Northern Ireland in 1981, only 6% of Catholics approved of violence to achieve political objectives, while in 1986 85% of Protestants and 96% of Catholics were opposed to the use of violence to protest the Anglo-Irish agreement (*Belfast Telegraph*, 16 January 1986). Within the Basque provinces the proportion supporting armed struggle has fluctuated between 3-8% (Clark, 1984, pp. 170-2). Although these percentages are low they still imply that a large number of people are willing to commit violence - enough to provide a steady stream of recruits to both groups. Furthermore, survey responses presumably underreport support for violence.

Not everybody who is a nationalist has a favorable image of national terrorists or approves of political violence. However, there is a tendency for the categories to overlap and to include the same kind of people. Within the ethnic constituency, class is not an important factor in affecting attitudes. What class differences exist can be explained by the class composition of the different ethnic groups. Thus, Northern Irish Catholics are disproportionately working class, so Irish nationalists are more likely to be working class, but ethnic Basques are disproportionately middle class so Basque nationalists are more likely to be middle class.

The high level of support for militant nationalism requires an explanation. Nationalist terrorists kill more people than do revolutionary terrorists, and are undoubtedly guilty of atrocities against civilians. Yet such atrocities do not discredit the cause for which they fight, nor tarnish their patriotic image. The most recent poll (MORI 1984) found 48% of Northern Irish Catholics agreeing that the IRA were patriots and idealists, virtually unchanged since 1978 (Moxon-Brown, 1981). Even the bombing of a Remembrance Day ceremony at Enniskillen resulted in only a 5% decline in those saying that they sympathized with the IRA (*Fortnight,* April 1988). One popular interpretation of militant nationalism sees it as a result of discrimination and deprivation. The difficulty with this argument is that most deprived minorities are not militant nationalists. The crucial factor seems to be political socialization. Militant nationalism is strong where people are taught to be militant nationalists. McCann (1974) provides a personal account of the process in his autobiography. Clark gives an excellent description of how young Basques become ETA members (1984, pp. 143-165). Given the existence of a militant nationalist ideology transmitted within the ethnic community, nationalist violence is legitimated. In their campaigns the IRA and ETA usually behave like patriots fighting a national liberation struggle. Their targets are predominantly military, and they rarely kill innocent civilians deliberately.[9]

Insurgent violence provokes repressive violence. Confronting an ethnic insurgency, the authorities adopt policies that impact upon all members of the ethnic community. In Northern Ireland, those arrested, interned, or shot by the security forces have been predominantly and disproportionately Catholic. Within Catholic areas, routine identity checks and house searches affect all the inhabitants, regardless of their politics or involvement in political violence. A similar situation obtains in Spain where Basque provinces have experienced the full rigors of Spanish counter insurgency policies. The result is widespread alienation among Catholics and Basques, and a polarization of attitudes towards security policy between Catholics and Protestants, Basques and non-Basques. Table 4 shows this polarization clearly. This polarization in its turn maintains support for the insurgents.

Table 4.4
Support for Security Measures by Country and Ethnic Group

Northern Ireland	Catholics	Protestants
British government should take a tougher line with IRA	55	95
Agree with Internment	5	52
Person gets fair trial in Northern Ireland	12	73
No Concessions to Hunger Strikers	38	97
Reintroduce death penalty for all terrorist murders	20	69
Shoot to kill terrorists	7	61
Approve plastic bullets	13	86
Hang terrorists	29	74

Spain	Basques	Rest of Spain
ETA are terrorists who should be pursued and eliminated	17	50
Don't accept demands or negotiate with terrorists	43	85

Sources: Moxon-Browne (1981), *Fortnight* 6 September 1974, Index to International Public Opinion (1981-2), BBC Spotlight (1985), *Belfast Telegraph* 6 February 1985, Clark (1984), Gunther, Sani and Shabad (1986)

Public opinion and revolutionary violence

The strategy of revolutionary terrorists is very different from that of nationalist insurgents. Their goal is to make a revolution and they believe that terrorism can be a catalyst in creating a revolutionary situation. Two processes supposedly produce revolutionary consciousness. In the nineteenth century, many anarchists and social revolutionaries believed that the masses would be inspired by the 'propaganda of the deed' to rise up against oppression. The Narodnaya Volya's manifesto claimed that 'terrorist activity..aims to undermine the prestige of the government, to demonstrate the possibility of struggle against the government (and) to arouse in this manner the revolutionary spirit of the people and their confidence in the success of their cause'. Kropotkin said that one terrorist act could 'make more propaganda than a thousand pamphlets. Above all, it awakens the spirit of revolt'. This view was echoed a century later by Latin American revolutionaries. Regis Debray wrote that 'the destruction of one troop transport truck is more effective propaganda for the local population than a thousand speeches'. According to the Tupamaros, 'revolutionary action in itself....generates revolutionary consciousness, organization and conditions' (Schmid and de Graf, 1982; Moss, 1972; Debray, 1967).

An alternative view of how to create a revolutionary situation is the 'provocation-repression' theory. By attacking the establishment and the security forces, the insurgents provoke the state into mass repression which alienates the general public, and increases support for the rebels. The Brazilian revolutionary, Marighella (1969) is one of the best-known advocates of this policy.

In addition to mobilizing and radicalizing their own potential supporters, revolutionary terrorists seek to destroy the morale of their enemies. For the Tupamaros 'intimidation and reprisals constituted an essential guerrilla tactic in that they can lead to the moral defeat of key components of the security forces or the government machine' (Porzecanski, 1973, pp. 45-6).

Revolutionary terrorists typically start off with a much smaller degree of popular support than nationalist terrorists. Only a small proportion favor revolutionary change. Survey data are available for Uruguay, Italy, Germany and Spain on general ideological orientations and their changes over time. In Uruguay the population was asked whether they believed the solution to the country's problems lay in 'armed revolution' or 'law and order'. In Germany and Italy the options were 'radical change by revolutionary action', 'gradual improvement by reforms' and 'valiant defense against all subversive forces'.

The public perception of revolutionary terrorists is less favorable than the public perception of nationalist terrorists. In Uruguay, respondents were asked whether the Tupamaros were well-intentioned revolutionaries or common delinquents. In Italy, the public was asked to choose one or two phrases that best applied to the Red Brigade members. Three phrases were negative (instruments controlled from on high, dangerous assassins or crazy) but the others were ambivalent (pursuing a just end with the wrong means) or very positive (fighting for a better society). In Germany the question was whether the Baader-Meinof gang 'acted out of political convictions or if they had now become true criminals'.

Table 4.5
Public Attitudes Towards Revolution

	Support Revolution	Positive Image	Approve Violence
Uruguay	12	34	-
Italy	13	28	2
Germany	2	18	1

Sources: *Indice Gallup de Opinion Publica* (1968), *Index to International Public Opinion* (1981-2), *L'Espresso* (10 January 1982), Weinberg and Eubank (1987), *Allensbach* (1971), Lodge (1988)

The Marxist rhetoric of revolutionary terrorists presumes that they will be supported by the working class. In fact the Tupamaros and Baader-Meinof are viewed most sympathetically by those of higher socioeconomic status. Demography rather than class is a differentiating factor with men somewhat more sympathetic then women, and the young noticeably more so than the old. A similar pattern is found in support for revolution.

Table 4.6
Percentage Holding Positive Image of Revolutionary Terrorists by
Class and Demographic Characteristics

	Baader-Meinhof	Tupamaros
Men	20	36
Women	16	33
Young	25	47
Middle Aged	16	35
Elderly	13	27
Educated	18	37
Less Educated	17	31
Upper Class	-	37
Middle Class	-	37
Lower Class	-	32

Sources: *Allensbacher Jahrbuch (1971)*, *Indice Gallup de Opinion Publica*, (1969-72).

The low level of support for revolution and revolutionary terrorists is easily explained. Modern Western societies are typically prosperous, with rising standards of living and well-developed systems of social welfare. Politically they are free and democratic. For the great mass of citizens therefore, demands for a revolutionary transformation of society are incomprehensible. In Uruguay and Italy, revolutionary attitudes were more prevalent than elsewhere because of economic decline and political instability. The Tupamaros emerged in a society with the highest rate of inflation and the lowest rate of growth in Latin America. Of all EEC countries, Italy had the highest percentage of those dissatisfied with 'the way that democracy is working in my country'. Germans on the other hand, had the highest degree of satisfaction with democracy, and the lowest percentage advocating revolution.

The only group in modern western society for whom millennial movements have a strong appeal are the university-educated in general, and students in particular.[10] Several explanations are offered for this phenomenon. Halperin (1976, p. 52) argues that universities produce an over-supply of liberal arts and social science graduates who are unable to find suitable employment. Revolutionary movements

> express the despair of young members of the administrative class radicalized and alienated from society by the deterioration of their prospects in countries of stagnant economy...In case of success the movements offer political power and a new role for the administrative class.

Other writers emphasize specific problems, faced by Italian and German students.

> Inadequate classroom and living facilities and a poor student-teacher ratio were the result of overcrowding. A more fundamental set of problems centered around the archaic nature of the university system' (Stohl, 1988, p. 418).

Some students became revolutionaries because they took their Professor's radical ideologies seriously.[11] Adorno plaintively remarked that 'I presented a theoretical model, how could I suspect that people would want to put it into effect with Molotov cocktails'.

Terrorist attacks clearly failed to generate a revolutionary mood in the general population. In Uruguay and Italy, where major left-wing campaigns were mounted, the number favoring revolution declined steadily throughout the period of terrorist activity. In Uruguay, the figure dropped from 12% in July 1968 to 1% in July 1972, while in Italy the decline was from 13% in November 1976 to 6% in October 1981. In Germany where leftist terrorism was conducted at a much lower level, the proportion of revolutionaries remained virtually unchanged at a trivial level.

Instead terrorism generated a backlash, with increased support for tough law and order measures. In Uruguay, Germany and Italy there is clear evidence of such a relationship. In Uruguay, the number of terrorist acts rose each year during 1968-72, and this is matched by a steady increase in the law and order category. The worst years for terrorism in Germany were 1977 and 1980, and in Italy 1978 and 1980, and during these years the percentage of the population favoring a 'valiant defense of society' reached a maximum.

These shifts in Italy and Germany can be compared to those found in the EEC bloc as a whole, to see whether the trend is due to a general change in political climate in the seventies. In fact, the trend in the other EEC countries is different. From November 1976 to April 1981, the average of the other EEC countries (excluding Germany and Italy) shows a slight increase in the proportion of revolutionaries (6% to 7%) and no change in the proportion favoring a valiant defence against subversion (27% at both dates) (IIPO, 1976-1981).

Attacks on public places produce fear and anger in the public. After the bombing of a Frankfurt department store, one German radical was exultant. 'A burning department store with burning people transmits for the first time in a major European city that stirring Vietnam feeling' (Stohl, 1988, p. 421). Ordinary Germans are unlikely to have shared such feelings. When nationalist terrorists kill soldiers their victims are foreigners, but in Italy and Germany when revolutionary terrorists killed policemen the working class identified with their victims (Clutterbuck, 1978, p. 38).

The Uruguayan situation is ambiguous, however, in that Tupamaro violence does not appear to have affected public perceptions of them. Since this assessment differs from the conventional wisdom, and since the data are exceptionally good, the Uruguayan case will be examined in more detail. In the early stages of their campaign, the Tupamaros carefully avoided unnecessary violence, and attacked only the rich and elite. During Christmas they hijacked a food truck and distributed the groceries in the slums of Montevideo. They robbed the casino, but returned that share which would have gone to the employees. They broke into a financial institution and publicized its corrupt and illegal practices (which implicated a cabinet minister). When one of their kidnap victims had a heart attack, they kidnapped a specialist to treat him, and then released their prisoner when his condition worsened.

Such tactics created a favorable image for the Tupamaros, but the public supposedly turned against them once they began to murder people, and they lost their original Robin Hood image as imaginative student pranksters who pilfered from the rich to give to the poor. This is a common view, usually supported by citing polls which show a dramatic decline in those thinking the Tupamaros were 'motivated by a concern for social justice' from 59 percent in 1971 to 4 percent in 1972.[12]

However, an analysis of the polls of Gallup Uruguay suggests a different conclusion. Three questions were asked repeatedly: whether a specific action was a legitimate revolutionary act or a crime; whether the Tupamaros were well-intentioned revolutionaries or common delinquents; and, whether there was any justification for the Tupamaros 'under the political conditions of the country'.

Some evidence does suggest that a soft-line campaign helps maintain a more favorable terrorist image. For example, the proportion of respondents who believed kidnappings to be legitimate revolutionary acts, increased after the victims were returned unharmed, as happened in the cases of Fly and Jackson. When Fly was first kidnapped only 18% of the individuals surveyed thought it a legitimate revolutionary act, but 32% saw it as such after he was released. In the case of Jackson[13] the figure rose from 30% to 36%. On the other hand, the killing of Mitrione brought about a dramatic decline in those thinking his abduction was justified. The week before his death, the public was evenly divided between those who thought it a legitimate revolutionary act (34%) and those who considered it a crime (34%). After his murder the division became 18% and 44%.

However, terrorist violence clearly has only a temporary effect. Figure 3, showing the proportion considering the Tupamaros 'well-intentioned revolutionaries' and their actions 'justified under the political conditions of the country', does not suggest any deterioration of their public image. The first killings of policemen were not until July 1969, but the public perception of them as well - intentioned revolutionaries averaged 38.7% before that date, compared to 38.9% afterwards.   Mitrione's murder had no discernable impact on public opinion either. Nor does the actual number of killings appear to be a negative factor. The percentage of respondents thinking the Tupamaros justified under the political conditions of the country increased substantially during the period when terrorist killings were at their highest.

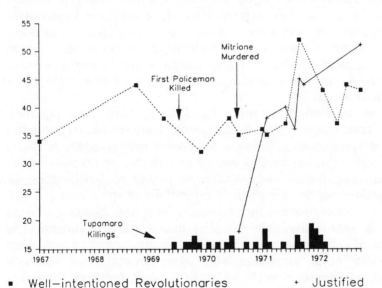

Figure 4.3 Attitudes Towards the Tupamaros

Source: *Indice Gallup de Opinion Publica* (1969-1972)

Why the public perceptions of the Tupamaros remained favorable, even though the proportion favoring revolution was declining, is difficult to explain. Perhaps public attitudes were affected by government countermeasures against the guerrillas.

The hope that terrorism would provoke the authorities into massive and indiscriminate repression, which would turn the public

⌈In all three countries governments did respond with repression to the outbreak of political violence. They declared a state of emergency, reduced civil liberties and gave special powers to the security forces. Large numbers were arrested or interned. People were stopped and questioned on the street, and their houses searched. Several, including some innocent of any participation in violence, were killed or wounded. However, for the most part the public approved of these tough measures.⌉

The crucial determinant of public attitudes to government security policies seems to be who was affected by them. In Italy and Germany, security measures affected the general public only temporarily and during clearly defined crises (such as the Moro and Schleyer kidnappings). At other times 'since the terrorists proclaim themselves to be revolutionary leftists, radical left wing groups are naturally suspect and become targets of intensive investigation and sometimes harassment by the security forces' (Mack, 1981). In Uruguay from mid-1970 onwards, mass searches and roadblocks affected the public at large, but most of those arrested and brutally interrogated were members of the left wing party, Frente Amplio.

In Italy and Germany, political leftists opposed government security policies, but constituted only a small percentage of the population - and were already radicalized. Working class supporters of the German SDP and the Italian PCI approved the policies to almost the same degree as those supporting the conservative parties.

In the case of Uruguay, opposition was more widespread. Moss (1972, p. 217) claims that 'emergency measures alienated public opinion'. Porzecanski (1973, pp. 55-6) claims the police 'became well known among the population for extensive and routine use of torture, as well as for heavy-handed citywide search operations'. These massive searches 'conducted clumsily at all hours of the night....created great resentment among Montevideo's population'. Labrousse (1973, p. 130) describes how 'the population was incensed by the continual police controls'. The fact that anti terrorist measures had more of an impact on the general public in Uruguay than elsewhere, may account for the noticeably lower degree of support for such measures. Thus, the public continued to regard the terrorists as well-intentioned revolutionaries' and 'justified under the political conditions of the country'.

Table 4.7
Support for Security Measures by Country and Party

Uruguay	COL	BLAN	FA	Total
Favor hardline with terrorists	35	23	7	22
Approve military courts for terrorists	64	55	20	48
Severe penalties justified	49	57	29	43
Suspension of individual guarantees justified	70	57	23	50
Approve emergency measures	74	53	15	43
Approve declaration of State of Internal War	84	55	33	55
Detention well-handled and justified	68	59	16	48
Identity checks and street searches unnecessary	87	80	39	70
Germany	SPD	FPD	CDU	Total
Stricter anti-terrorism laws needed	64	85	60	71
More severe penalties for acts of terrorism	-	-	-	86
Death Penalty for terrorists	52	43	60	55
Terrorists received fair trial at Stammheim	60	66	68	60
No blame to authorities in Hunger strikers' death	75	77	85	77
Willing to give up personal freedoms to fight terrorism	55	53	66	60
Accept house searches to fight terrorism	62	40	72	69

Table 4.7 (Continued)

Italy	DP	PCI	PSI	DC	Total
More severe penalties for acts of terrorism	-	-	-	-	87
Police should act with force and decision	11	45	45	78	65

Allensbach (1968-1978)
Index to International Public Opinion (1979-83)
Fabris (1977)

Notes

1. This chapter concentrates on the relationship between terrorism and public opinion because terrorists deliberately use political violence to produce certain effects. Rioting is often interpreted as a manifestation of public resentments and frustration - for example, black rioters in the 1960s were said to be 'sending a message to American society' (Dynes and Quarantelli, 1968). However riots are obviously not planned in the same way that terrorist acts are.

2. The September 1975 execution of two ETA guerrillas, one of ethnic Basque descent, the second of Spanish immigrant parents was celebrated in a book (*The Wind and the Roots*) as symbolizing the two elements of the Basque nation. Clark (1984, p. 147) shows that a significant and increasing proportion of ETA's membership is of mixed or Spanish background. The PNV takes a more restrictive cultural and linguistic definition of Basque identity than ETA does.

3. Unfortunately since no polls could be found, I was unable to analyze public attitudes towards rightwing terrorism. However, it is generally agreed that right-wing terrorism is more feared by the man in the street because, unlike left-wing terrorism which is directed against members of the elite, their indiscriminate bombings kill and wound large numbers of ordinary people. In Italy and Spain, neo-fascist violence received significant media coverage - all of it negative.

4. A statewide survey by Jimenez Blanco (1977) on regional consciousness found that Barcelona and the Basque country expressed the most acute grievances over administrative centralization, were most likely to support independence and were the most likely to vote for separatist parties.

5. On the basis of their names, only 30 out of 403 victims of terrorism in the Basque provinces appear to have been ethnic Basques.

6. In the five years before the survey (1978-83) 61 Catholics and 199 Protestants were victims of terrorism. Thus Protestants who make up 63% of the population, suffered 76% of the deaths.

7. From 1974-77 those favoring troop withdrawal averaged 57%, and from 1978-81 those wanting to withdraw the troops

troops immediately or within five years also averaged 57%. See Rose, McAllister and Mair (1978) for figures before 1977 and *Index to International Public Opinion* for later figures.

8. See Gunther, Sani and Shabad (1986, p. 362). Earlier polls by Linz in 1978 and 1979 show a decline in those supporting negotiation or acceptance of terrorist demands from 24% to 17% (Gordenker, 1980, p. 48). (Clark ,1990, p. 224) cites more recent polls in 1987-8 which found that a 'clear majority favor a negotiated end to the struggle'.

9. Legitimate military or political targets constitute 80% of ETA's victims and 65% of the IRA's victims.

10. On the political alienation and radicalism of German and Italian students see Alexander and Gleason (1981, pp. 256-82) and Weinberg and Eubank (1987, p. 36).

11. On the ambivalent relationship between leftist intellectuals and the terrorists see the essays by Pridham and Furlong in Lodge (1981).

12. The often cited poll showing a decline in public support for the Tupamaros is due to errors by both Crozier and Clutterbuck. See Hewitt (1990) for details.

13. Claude Fly, an American agricultural expert was kidnapped in 1970 and Geoffrey Jackson, the British consul in 1971.

5 The Politics of Public Order

This chapter considers the political consequences of political violence. It examines how politicians respond to threats to public order, and how partisan divisions and political stability are affected. In order to analyze the politics of public order, all actions by elected politicians, party officials or political appointees pertaining to political violence and the maintenance of law and order were recorded and coded. The sources used were *Keesings International Archives* and the *New York Times*. In addition the biweekly news digest, *Latin America,* was examined in order to produce the Uruguayan chronology. Almost everything that politicians do falls into one of four categories: executive actions, legislation, meetings and statements. The totals for each country, classified by type, are presented in Table 1.

Table 5.1
Political Acts on Public Order Issues by Country

	Germany	Italy	Spain	Uruguay	Ulster
Legislation	24	27	27	26	19
Executive Action	43	48	65	37	75
Statement	74	85	93	69	578
Meeting	12	10	12	8	71
Other	2	4	4	3	14
	155	174	201	143	757

There are significant differences between the five societies in how violence affected their politics. In Germany, Italy and Spain violence was a political problem - often a serious one - but did not result in a transformation of the political system as it did in Uruguay and Northern Ireland. In Uruguay in response to the Tupamaro campaign liberal democracy was supplanted by more authoritarian practices. The role of the military increased and in June 1973 the legislature was dissolved and a military-dominated regime set up. In Northern Ireland, communal rioting and terrorism by both republicans and loyalists led to the abolition of the Northern Irish Parliament (Stormont) in March 1972, and direct rule by London. Since then the province has remained in a political limbo, intermittently interrupted by various abortive constitutional initiatives. Presumably these different outcomes should be reflected in the political process itself. Therefore in the analysis, the three stable polities will be considered first, and then Northern Ireland and Uruguay will be examined to see how they differed from them.

The stable polities: Germany, Italy and Spain

The political parties in all three countries can be distributed along a left-right spectrum. In Spain ethnic-regional cleavages provide an additional source of partisan division. The party system was highly fractionalized in Italy and Spain, far less so in Germany.[1] Table 2 shows the distribution of seats by party in each country for the election prior to the outbreak of violence.

Table 5.2
Distribution of Seats by Party Classified by Ideology (%)

	Germany 1969		Italy 1968		Spain	
Extreme Left			PCI	28	PCE	6
			PSIUP	4	PSP	2
Moderate Left	SDP	45	PSU	14	PSOE	34
					PDC	3
Center	FDP	6	PRI	1	PNV	2
					UCD	46
Moderate Right	CDU	49	DC	42		
			PLI	5	AP	
Extreme Right			MSI	5		5

*Parties with less than 1% of seats not shown

Throughout the period, Germany was ruled by a center-left, Italy by a center-right coalition. In Germany the Social Democratic Party (SDP) was the dominant partner in coalition with the Free Democratic Party (FDP). In Italy the Christian Democrats (DC) were the main governing party, but depended upon support from a number of small parties which were usually represented in the cabinet. The growing strength of the Communist Party (PCI) finally led to the 'historic compromise' of May 1968 in which the PCI agreed to support the Christian Democratic government in return for representation on various official bodies. The willingness of the PCI to accept the legitimacy of bourgeois democracy produced a crisis for many Marxists. A number of extreme leftists split from the PCI and contested the elections under various labels (Il Manifesto, Party of Proletarian Unity, Proletarian Democracy, New Left Union). A new radical party (PR) was formed in 1976 emphasizing civil liberties.

In Spain the first democratic post-Franco elections in 1977 and 1979 resulted in a victory for the Union of the Democratic Center (UCD). However, the party lacked ideological cohesion and split into several factions by the time of the 1982 elections. The disintegration of the UCD produced a realignment in which the rightist Popular Alliance (AP) became the main opposition party, while the Socialists (PSOE) surged to victory.

Public order as an issue

The total number of political acts plotted over time (see figures 1-3), serves as an indicator of the rise and decline of public order as an issue. The amount of political attention paid to law-and-order issues can be explained in three ways; as a justified reaction to a real threat, as a response to public concern, and as a result of elite manipulation of the political agenda.

Some matters force themselves on to the political agenda. Governments cannot ignore kidnappings or murders of high ranking officials, nor other spectacular atrocities. The figures clearly show that the amount of political concern is closely linked to such events, and to the general level of terrorist activity.

Law and order issues have a high salience for the general public. According to Budge and Farlie (1983, p. 49) 'when a breakdown of public order is threatened, more citizens are likely to feel more affected personally than by any other type of issue'. Not surprisingly there is a general congruence between public concern over law and order, and the amount of political attention it attracts.

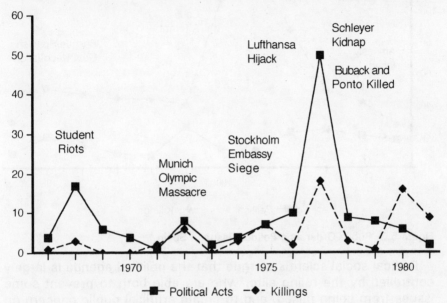

Figure 5.1 Public Order as a Political Issue in Germany

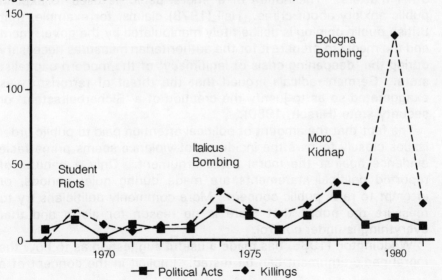

Figure 5.2 Public Order as a Political Issue in Italy

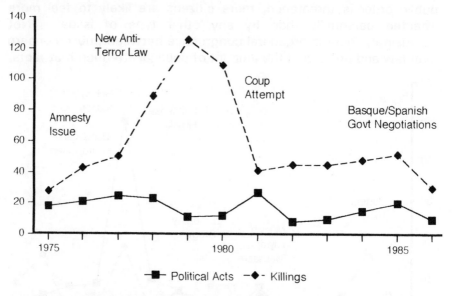

Figure 5.3 Public Order as a Political Issue in Spain

Radical social scientists argue that the political agenda is largely controlled by the ruling elite, who are able both to prevent some issues from being raised, and to create artificial public concern on other matters. The notion of a 'moral panic' is used to explain public anxiety about crime. Hall (1978) claims, for example, that British public opinion is deliberately manipulated by the government and the media to prepare it for the authoritarian measures necessary during the 'deepening crisis of legitimacy' of the modern capitalist state. German radicals argued that the threat of terrorism was exaggerated so as to justify the creation of a 'Sicherheitsstaat' or security state (Hirsch, 1980).

The fact that the amount of political attention paid to public order issues closely follows the incidence of violence seems prima facie evidence against the moral panic argument. Only a handful of reported political statements are made during quiet periods, or attempt to raise public concern. More commonly politicians try to reassure the public that there is no reason for alarm and that everything is under control.

Waddington (1986) has made a useful suggestion as to how the moral panic argument can be tested. Implicit in the concept of a moral panic is the claim that public reaction is unjustified by the scale of the problem. Therefore, we can compare the amount of political attention paid to different issues, to see whether the concern evoked on a particular issue is so disproportionate as to justify the moral panic label. Since radicals usually consider rightist or fascist violence to be a genuine threat, Table 3 shows the number of political acts concerned with right wing violence and the number concerned with left wing violence, in relation to the number of deaths caused by each.

Clearly the data do not show that politicians exaggerate the danger from the left. If anything they seem more sensitive to the threat posed by right-wing extremism. Given the history of all three countries, this is an understandable response, but not what the moral panic hypothesis predicts.

Table 5.3
Relative Concern Expressed Over Leftist and Rightist Violence

| | Germany | | Italy | | Spain | |
	Leftist Violence	Rightist Violence	Leftist Violence	Rightist Violence	Leftist Violence	Rightist Violence
Political Acts	28	18	30	38	43	29
Deaths	33	13	131	186	501	25
Ratio	0.8	1.4	0.2	0.2	0.1	1.2

Conflict and consensus

Although a growing literature shows that political parties differ in their policies on many issues, the effective working of democracy also requires a degree of bipartisan consensus and a willingness not to over-emphasize conflict. Thus both in Germany (Von Behme, 1984) and in Italy (Cazzola, 1974; DiPalma, 1977) there is a high degree of legislative cooperation between ideologically opposed parties.

The issue of how to deal with political violence could be expected to produce either conflict or competition between parties. On the one hand, when political violence is aimed at destroying the system

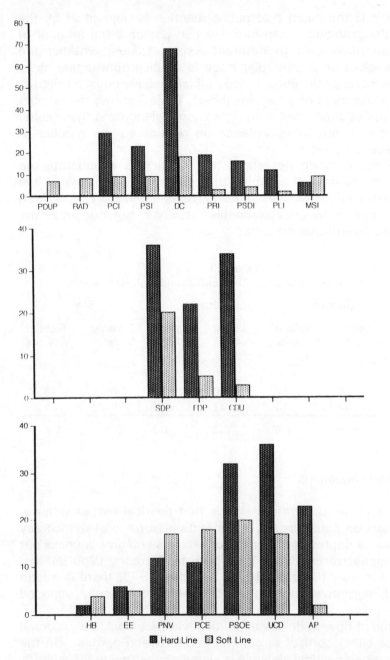

Figure 5.4 Party Attitudes To Public Order in Italy, Germany and Spain

itself, political opponents may unite to defend democracy, since they all feel threatened by extremism. On the other hand, attitudes to law and order involve deeply rooted ideological differences, over which it is difficult to compromise. Also given the salience of these issues to the public, political parties are tempted to 'play politics' in the hope of winning votes.

A simple measure of conflict/consensus can be constructed by counting the number of times that politicians agree and disagree. Agreement exists whenever politicians vote the same way on legislation, take the same position on an issue, make supportive statements or meet with one another. Disagreement occurs when politicians vote differently on legislation, take opposed positions, or make statements critical of one another. This measure is a crude one, in that it treats all disagreements as equivalent, and disregards both the intensity of, and the subject over which the disagreement occurs. However, the procedure does indicate the overall pattern of inter-party relationships. In all three countries, agreement was far more usual than disagreement. Of the total number of party alignments 64% in Italy, 73% in Germany and 75% in Spain involved parties agreeing or cooperating with one another.

Only a few small parties found themselves outside this consensus. In Italy, extreme leftists, the Radicals and the neofascist MSI had more disagreements than agreements with the other parties.[2] The Radicals were so concerned about civil liberties, that they usually objected to the anti-terrorist legislation, supported by the major parties. The ultraleft's ambivalence was summed up by the slogan 'ne con lo stato ne con le BR' (neither with the state nor with the Red Brigades). The MSI, the pariah of Italian politics, was accused of being fascist and of inciting violence. The Minister of the Interior even accused them of killing policemen. Several times, parliament voted to withdraw the parliamentary immunity of MSI deputies so that they could be prosecuted. In Spain, the two radical Basque nationalist parties (Herri Batasuna and Euzkadiko Ezkerra) were usually to be found in opposition to the main Spanish parties. However, after the granting of autonomy to the Basque region Euzkadiko Ezkerra became more supportive of the status quo, and currently is part of the consensus. Most of the time, parties agreed with those parties which were ideologically close to them, and were most likely to disagree with those ideologically distant from them. Thus the political cleavages and alignments resulting from law and order issues were similar to those found in other political issues.

Why parties disagree

Partisan divisions over the law and order issue are not merely polemical. They are based upon genuine and substantive disagreements as to the nature of the problem and how to deal with it. In criticizing one another and making political statements, the political parties take positions on the issue. For the most part, these positions can be characterized as either 'hard' or 'soft'. Statements that terrorism must be fought vigorously, that no concessions should be made to terrorists, calling for severe punishments such as the death penalty, or advocating that special emergency powers be given to police and judges are considered hardline. Calls for police restraint, pleas for understanding the social causes of violence, warnings that the government is overreacting and expressing concern that civil liberties are endangered are classified as softline.

One would expect marked differences in the number of hard and soft positions taken by different parties, and figure (4) shows that this is indeed the case. In general, politicians are much more likely to express hard-line rather than soft line views. This is true for almost all parties, both those on the right and also for those on the left, such as the Italian PCI and the German SDP. In Spain, the PSOE, after it became the governing party in 1982, proved to be as hardline in its policies towards ETA as the previous UCD governments had been. The exceptions fall into two groups; parties on the extreme left such as the Italian Proletarian Democrats (PDUP) and the Spanish Communists, and nationalist parties based on ethnic minorities, such as the Basque PNV and HB.

Partisan differences, however, are revealed in the willingness to take soft line positions. Left wing politicians are far more likely to express liberal opinions. These patterns can be explained as a result of the interplay between party ideology and electoral considerations. Survey data show that public attitudes on such matters are generally correlated with left-right partisanship, but that the distribution is skewed in favor of hard-line policies (i.e many voters who normally support left wing parties support tough law and order positions). For Rightist politicians both party ideology and a desire to win votes coincide, and lead to a clear and emphatic hard-line stance. For leftist politicians the situation is more difficult. Since party activists and legislators are usually very liberal on civil liberties, this creates a dilemma.[3] The parties respond by sending a mixed message - get tough on terrorist and rioters but respect civil liberties and political freedoms.

The SDP leadership in Germany often made such statements. Brandt, in 1968, reassured the public that the SDP would ensure that the emergency powers for which they had just voted would not be abused. Schmidt, in 1975, declared that the government 'must be prepared to go to the limits of what the free constitutional state allows'. An almost identical statement was made by the Italian Minister of the Interior, Cossiga, in 1977. The government, he promised, would maintain law and order by 'all preventive and repressive means which the law allows'. This strategy should minimize both electoral losses and internal party opposition. However, since the law and order issue does put the Left at a disadvantage, one would expect attempts on their part to de-emphasize the issue, while parties of the Right should try to raise the issue and call for more severe policies.

This was very much the case in Germany, where SDP leaders Schmidt and Brandt repeatedly warned against over-reacting. At Buback's funeral, Schmidt claimed that the terrorists were 'seeking to produce an emotional and uncontrolled reaction', and on another occasion cautioned against 'law and order hysteria'. Brandt urged that the Munich massacre not be turned into an election issue, and made the same appeal after the Oktoberfest bombing. He could not 'imagine responsible politicians wanting to run in an election campaign with...terrorists'.

Parties in addition to taking different policy positions can criticize how policies are carried out, claiming that the government is incompetent. In Spain during the 1979 election campaign, PSOE criticisms of the ruling UCD focused on the 'high levels of unemployment and inflation and the governments inability to end terrorist violence' (Gunther, Sani, and Shabad ,1986, p. 281). To an extent the government can protect against this by bringing the opposition into the decision-making process, as the SDP government did in Germany and as the Christian Democratic Party did in Italy. However, even when there is high-level consultation, opposition parties still try to score points if governments make mistakes. In Germany, the Christian Democratic Opposition blamed the government for the suicides of imprisoned terrorists, and the FDP Minister of the Interior was forced to resign over the bugging scandal. The Italian PCI accused the government of inertia and of failing in the battle against terrorism. They raised the issue of right wing plots in the security services, and urged a parliamentary probe. When Donat-Cattin, a terrorist suspect and the son of a Christian Democratic politician, fled his imminent arrest, it was alleged that his father had been tipped off by Prime Minister Cossiga. This scandal was exploited by the PCI, who repeatedly called for Cossiga's impeachment.

Politicians may disagree as to who is responsible for violence and the breakdown of public order. Does the danger come mainly from extremists of the right or extremists of the left? Are demonstrations justified or unjustified? Do peaceful protests turn violent because of heavy-handed police tactics or because there was a conspiracy to provoke trouble? One might expect partisan considerations to lead to a situation in which leftist politicians blame right wing extremists and vice versa. However, Table 4 which lists those who are blamed for political violence by party and country, reveals a more complex pattern.

In some cases politicians do concentrate on political violence by their ideological enemies; for example, the MSI, CDU and AP focused on leftist terrorists and rioters. However, in as many cases political parties attack their 'own' extremists. Thus the PCI and PSOE attacked leftist terrorism, and the PNV and EE attacked ETA. Such attacks are a means of dissociating themselves from the terrorists, and therefore a defense against accusations that they are sympathetic to the extremists. Such accusations are not uncommon. Governments may be accused of bias, acting against one group of extremists but ignoring violence perpetrated by the other side. At its worst, politicians may claim that their opponents encourage violence by their inflammatory rhetoric, or even that they justify or advocate extremist violence. This kind of criticism is likely to occur only in societies where strong ethnic and ideological cleavages exist.

The MSI was attacked by all the other Italian parties for instigating violence, and was accused of wanting to reconstitute fascism. On five separate occasions, the parliamentary immunity of MSI politicians was lifted so that they could be tried on such charges. Allegations of bias surfaced on several occasions. In 1971, the PCI and PSI claimed that leaks about leftist terrorist strength were timed to divert attention from neo-fascist plots. A PSDI official retorted that the PCI exaggerated the fascist danger in order to justify leftist violence. In 1975, politicians of the Right and Center focused on left wing terrorism, while Leftist politicians claimed that terrorism was a provocation intended to stir up a law-and-order backlash, a tool to discredit the Left, or even that terrorists claiming to be leftists were really neo-fascists. In Germany during a 1970 debate, the SDP whip accused the CDU of 'stirring the murder lust of right wing extremists', while in 1981, after the Oktoberfest bombings, Strauss attacked the FDP Minister of the Interior for the 'development of an atmosphere in which atrocities occur'.

Table 5.4

Who Was Blamed for Violence by Party %

	Right Wing Extremists	Left Wing Extremists	Police, Judiciary Security Services	Undefined Extremists/ Both Sides
ITALY				
MSI	25	50	0	25
DC	43	19	17	17
PRI	63	25	12	0
PSDI	57	29	0	14
PSI	36	21	29	14
PCI	23	59	9	9
Leftists	0	0	100	0
GERMANY				
CDU	22	67	6	0
FDP	38	38	8	0
SDP	32	39	7	0
SPAIN				
AP	22	56	0	22
UCD	44	29	6	21
PSOE	28	45	10	17
PCE	18	18	27	36
PNV	18	64	0	18
EE	0	83	0	17
HB	0	33	67	0

Uruguay: a revolutionary situation?

Uruguayan politics were dominated by the Blancos and Colorados. Traditionally these represented the split between the conservative rural sector and the more liberal population of Montevideo. However, these ideological labels are not particularly useful in analyzing the situation in the 1960s, since each party contained liberal and conservative elements. In addition to the Blancos and Colorados, a handful of more radical leftwing parties (Communists, Socialists and Christian Democrats) took a small share of the vote. In late 1970 a new political alignment, the Frente Amplio, emerged. This 'broad front' included Communists, Socialists, Christian Democrats and some of the more radical Colorados.

Public order first became an issue in the late 1960s when growing militancy by students and workers led the government to resort to repression. Using the 'Medidas Prontas de Seguridad' (Prompt Security Measures), the President ordered the militarization of striking workers, censored newspapers and banned several small leftist and anarchist groups. As the Tupamaro campaign escalated, with kidnappings of political and business leaders, the issue became even more important. Finally in 1972, after a state of internal war was declared, the army crushed the Tupamaros. During this latter period, public order issues dominated the political scene.

The period was marked by confrontation between the executive and the legislature. Time and again, the President (first Pacheco and then Bordaberry) was opposed by a hostile Congress. Out of a total of 45 presidential/congressional interactions during the period, 37 (82%) involved Congress voting against a presidential request or criticizing some executive action. Sometimes this aligned all three parties Blancos, Colorados and the Frente Amplio against the President. For example in July 1971, the Chamber of Deputies voted 55 to 2 to impeach Pacheco, and with a similar show of agreement in March 1972, rejected Bordaberry's new draft security law and at the same time voted 67 to 1 to lift the existing emergency measures.

Although such virtual unanimity was exceptional, opposition to the President was almost as likely to come from his own Colorado party as from the opposition Blancos or the left wing Frente Amplio. Given the recurrent cleavage between executive and legislature, divisions by party became less important. Furthermore, both

Colorados and Blancos were divided into distinct factions with different ideologies and policy views. Thus the Colorado faction led by Senator Vasconcellos often voted against the President, while the conservative Blancos (led by Echegoyan) gave him crucial support on several occasions.

Table 5.5
Political Alignments in Uruguay (1967-73)

President and Legislature Opposed

Opposition from Blancos	10
Opposition from All Parties	8
Opposition from Blancos and Colorados	8
Opposition from Colorados	4
Opposition from Blancos and Leftists	3
Opposition from Leftists	2
Other	2

President and Legislature Agree

Support from Blancos	5
Support from Blancos and Colorados	1
Support from All Parties	1
Support from Leftists	1

Alignments Within Legislature

Blancos and Colorados Agree	3
Blancos and Leftists Agree	2
All parties agree	2
Colorados and Leftists Agree	1
Blancos Against Leftists	2
Other	3

The nature of the political criticism reveals a deeply divided polity. There was widespread opposition to the President's repressive policies by legislators of all parties. The restriction of civil liberties was consistently attacked by the Blanco leader, Wilson Ferreira Aldunate, and eventually even the conservative faction led by Echegoyan ended its support for the security measures just before the 1971 election.

Police incompetence and corruption provided an easy target for critics. The interior minister was forced to resign in April 1970, following the escape of a group of female Tupamaro prisoners.

(They were able to get out because the door was unlocked!) Police officers, authorized under the emergency powers to requisition vehicles, seized luxury cars so that their wives could use them to go shopping. Another mass escape in September 1971 offered further opportunities for the opposition to mock the President and the interior ministry. Allegations of torture by police led to a Senate Commission of Inquiry, headed by the dissident Colorado Senator Amilcar Vasconcellos. The commission, composed of both Colorados and Blancos, concluded unanimously that 'inhuman torture' including electric shocks, cigarette burns and psychological pressure was used routinely on Tupamaros, common criminals and innocents alike.

This was soon followed by the charge that President Pacheco had personally ordered the killing of three Tupamaros captured after they raided the town of Pando in October 1969. This sensational allegation was coupled with the claim that, in the same incident, the police had stolen several million pesos captured with the Tupamaros. These charges were to have been published in the Blanco newspaper, *El Debate,* and in order to prevent this, the government closed down the paper for five days in June 1970. The Interior Minister responded by calling the charges 'deliberate lies by a wretched little blackguard which only served the purpose of subversive organizations'.

As the security forces became more repressive, legislative criticism intensified. In April 1972, the President of the Chamber of Deputies was taken by the Tupamaros to hear the confession of a police photographer, Nelson Bardesio, whom they had taken prisoner. The politician said he accepted Bardesio's story that right-wing death squads had been set up by forces within the Ministry of the Interior. Similar accounts of death squad links to police were again publicized by opposition legislation in June 1972. A month later, after a left wing activist had been tortured to death by an army interrogation unit, Congress passed a resolution calling for those responsible to be named and punished.

Several times it was suggested that negotiation not repression was the appropriate policy for dealing with the Tupamaros. Heber, a Blanco leader, suggested in early 1971 that the government should negotiate with the Tupamaros not just over the release of hostages but on broad questions of national policy. In a similar vein, Ferreira proposed in mid 1972 that the solution to political violence lay in tackling the country's deep-rooted economic and social problems. Seregni, the leader of the Frente Amplio, claimed that 'It is not repression that is needed, but the removal of the problem's basic roots'.

The government and their supporters counterattacked by accusing the Frente Amplio of being linked to the Tupamaros. This accusation was denied strenuously by the Frente Amplio, but their sensitivity on the issue suggests that the charge had some impact. There were only isolated criticisms of Tupamaro violence. The Christian Democratic newspaper, *Ahora,* in an April 1971 editorial accused them of bearing major responsibility for the constitutional crisis. Following the death of a bus driver during a shootout between Tupamaros and soldiers in July 1972, the Communist party condemned the guerrillas for the first time. Categorizing politicians in terms of whether they took 'hard' or 'soft' positions on public order makes it clear that the cleavage was between executive and legislative rather than between parties.

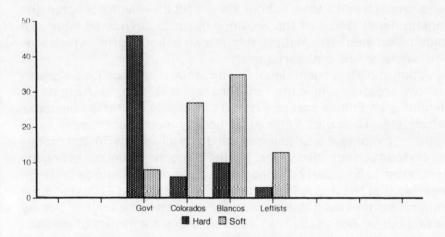

Figure 5.5 Party Attitudes To Public Order in Uruguay

A similar degree of polarization can be seen in who is blamed for violence. The government blamed the Tupamaros, the unions and striking workers, the legislators usually blamed the security forces and warned of the dangers of a military coup.

Table 5.6
Who Was Blamed for Violence by Political Group in Uruguay (%)

Who Blamed by:	Government	Colorados	Blancos	Leftists
Soviet Union	3	-	-	-
Union/Workers	14	-	-	-
Students	3	-	-	-
Tupamaros	69	-	-	
Both sides	3	-	9	33
Security forces	7	100	82	50
Death Squads	-	-	9	17

Northern Ireland: an unresolvable ethnic conflict

The main political cleavage in Northern Ireland prior to the emergence of the civil rights movement was between the Nationalists whose goal was a united Ireland, and the Unionists who defended the union with Britain. The only other important parties were the Northern Irish Labour Party (NILP) which accepted the constitutional status of the province but also advocated labor and trade union interests, and the Republican Labour party, which was both socialist and anti-partitionist.

Voting statistics are misleading indicators of party political support for two reasons; militant republicans refused to participate in elections, and those parties that did participate contested elections selectively. Thus Irish Nationalists usually restricted themselves to Catholic majority constituencies, and the Unionists in turn rarely contested such constituencies. Furthermore the Nationalists and the Republican Labour party divided the Catholic constituencies between them, so that the Republican Labour party dominated Belfast and the Nationalists the rest of the province. Fortunately the Loyalty Survey carried out by Rose (1971) in 1968 provides a measure of partisan identity broken down by religion. The survey shows that prior to the outbreak of communal violence 79% of the Protestants were Unionists and 11% supported the NILP. Fifty one per cent of the Catholics were Nationalists and 27% for the NILP. Only a handful of Catholics (5%) were Unionists and a minuscule 0.5% of the Protestants were Nationalists.

Party cohesion was weak and a large number of independents and unofficial candidates stood at every election. Factions of the same ideological tendency ran under varying labels in different elections. The parliament elected in 1965 had 38 Unionists, 9 Nationalists, 2 Republican Labour, 1 National Democrat[4] and 2 NILP.

The civil rights campaign had important consequences for both the Catholic/Nationalist bloc and the Protestant/Unionist bloc. The belief that they were discriminated against was widespread within the Catholic community and served to unite Catholics who held divergent views on partition, socialism and other issues. In the 1969 election three civil rights activists (Hume, Cooper and O'Hanlon) defeated three incumbent Nationalist MPs. Subsequently they joined with three other Catholic MPs who had been active in the civil rights campaign to form the Social Democratic and Labour party (SDLP). The SDLP became the main political party on the Catholic side, and were virtually unchallenged until the 1982 election in which Provisional Sinn Fein put up candidates for the first time.

While the civil rights issue increased political cohesion among Catholics, it fragmented the Unionist Party. The Rev. Ian Paisley opposed the reform policies of the Unionist Party leader O'Neill in the 1960s, and formed the Democratic Unionist Party (DUP) to express his policies. The Vanguard Unionist Party (VUP) was formed in 1973 under the leadership of William Craig, a hardline member of O'Neill's cabinet. However, VUP became more centrist in its policies and quickly lost support. The original Unionist party renamed itself the official Unionist Party (OUP) in 1973, and consisted, at that time, of those who supported Brian Faulkner as leader and were willing to accept the principle of 'Power sharing' between the Protestants and Catholics. The power sharing executive fell apart in May 1974 because of Protestant resistance to the proposed Council of Ireland. This led to a further split within the OUP, in which the small minority who continued to support Faulkner became the Unionist Party of Northern Ireland (UPNI). The NILP was badly damaged by the growth of communal tensions between working class Protestants and Catholics. However, a new non-sectarian grouping, the Alliance Party emerged in 1970.

The question of public order is connected to most other political issues in Northern Ireland because the national-constitutional question, which dominated Northern Irish politics, is at the root of the conflict between Nationalists and Unionists. However in examining public order as a political issue, I have restricted the analysis to those political acts dealing specifically with violence and political order.[5]

Since 1968, the question of political violence has dominated the political agenda. Although there is a rough correspondence between the level of violence and the amount of attention which it receives, this correlation is overlaid by a series of crises - such as the Hunger Strike.

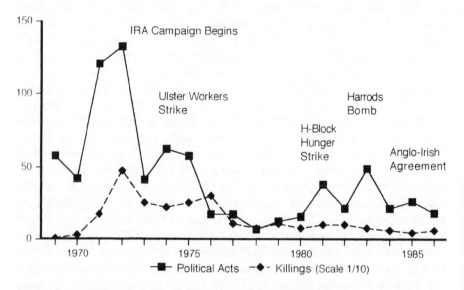

Figure 5.6 Public Order as a Political Issue in Northern Ireland

Northern Irish politics is played out on at least two levels - that of Northern Ireland itself and that of the United Kingdom as a whole.[6] As regards the Ulster parties, we find that Nationalists and Unionists were extremely polarized over security issues, with Unionists almost invariably taking a hard line and Nationalists a soft line. This pattern was repeated over and over again.

During the civil rights disturbances, Nationalists criticized the police, the Unionists defended them. Nationalists condemned the Special Powers Act, the Unionists wanted these emergency powers to be used. Although Nationalists at first welcomed the arrival of British troops, within months they were accusing the Army of shooting down Catholic civilians in cold blood. When two Catholic men in Londonderry were shot (July 1971) the SDLP withdrew from Stormont, and set up an 'Alternative Assembly'. After 'Bloody

Sunday' when troops shot dead 13 demonstrators, Hume called the action 'cold blooded murder', and Bernadette Devlin was so enraged that she physically attacked the Conservative Home Secretary in the House of Commons. Unionists, however, urged that the troops be more vigorous in their pursuit of terrorists. Paisley in his first speech to the British House of Commons charged that 'men and women were being slaughtered on the streets of Belfast because British soldiers failed to protect them'. When the British government set up a commission to examine Nationalist allegations that internees were being brutally treated during interrogation, Unionists denounced the commission as 'appeasement of the terrorists'.

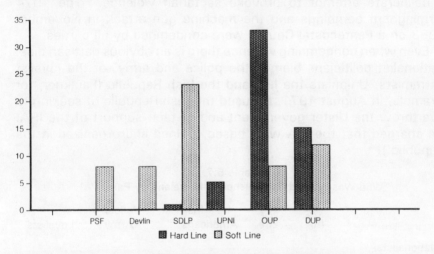

Figure 5.7 Party Attitudes To Public Order in Northern Ireland

Internment itself produced the most bitter division with the SDLP calling for civil disobedience and refusing to participate in constitutional discussions with the British government until the policy was ended. Unionists, for the most part, supported internment as an effective means of dealing with the IRA. The SDLP favored negotiations with the IRA, the Unionist parties were opposed. The SDLP wanted concessions made to the hunger strikers, the Unionists opposed any concessions.[7] DUP favored capital punishment for terrorists, the SDLP was opposed.

Counting the number of times that Unionists and Nationalists displayed consensus rather than conflict it is clear that situations producing agreement were rare. Eighty two per cent of the times the two groups disagreed or criticized one another. Even the statistics on the number of acts which were coded as showing consensus is probably an overestimate. First, although meetings are considered to indicate agreement, many meetings between Ulster politicians involved the two hostile groups in conference with a third party - usually the British government. Second, some instances in which the two sides agreed involved mutual denunciations of some terrorist atrocity. Thus both Nationalists and Unionists condemned the murder of three teenage soldiers in early 1971. In late 1971 both the SDLP and the Unionists charged that IRA bombings were a deliberate attempt to provoke sectarian violence. The 1974 Birmingham bombings and the machine gun attack in November 1983 on a Pentecostal Church were condemned by all parties.

Even when condemning violence there is an obvious partisan bias. Nationalist politicians blamed the police and army, or the loyalist extremists, Unionists the IRA and the Irish Republic (Faulkner, for example, in August 1971, accused the Irish Republic of seeking to overthrow the Ulster government and of tacit support of the IRA. He charged that the IRA was 'based, trained and organized in the Republic').

Table 5.7
Who Was Blamed for Violence in N. Ireland by Party (%)

	IRA	Eire	Irish Americans	Police/ Army	Loyalists
Nationalists/ SDLP	4	4	-	67	19
Unionists	71	20	5	2	-
Alliance	50	-	-	-	-
Conservatives	58	3	14	-	25
Labour	44	-	-	6	33

*Undefined extremists were blamed in the remaining cases.

Also support for tough security measures seems to depend on who they are directed against. Paisley, for example, was originally against internment on the grounds that it would be used against Protestant extremists, and several Unionist politicians favored concessions to loyalist prisoners. In a similar fashion, Hume and Devlin called for increased security measures when Catholics were victims of loyalist terrorism in 1973.

Disagreements were intense and often couched in extremist rhetoric. Chichester-Clark described the civil rights disturbances as 'violence by a conspiracy of forces seeking to overthrow Northern Ireland', and described the civil rights leaders as 'political streetwalkers'. Another Unionist MP accused Bernadette Devlin of using the money she raised in the United States to buy weapons. Craig, in March 1972, called on loyalists to 'liquidate their enemies'. Nationalist politicians were equally strident. Devlin said that Catholic barricades would 'come down when the government falls'. During a tense period in 1969, Nationalist MPs charged that Protestants were planning genocide against the Catholic population (*New York Times*, 18 August 1969). This is not to ignore the fact that within each group one can distinguish between moderates and extremists. DUP tended to advocate more hardline policies than the OUP. Paisley, on one occasion, called for the use of 'the mailed fist' against Catholic rioters, and frequently accused the Unionist government of weakness and appeasement. On the Nationalist side, Bernadette Devlin consistently took a more militant position than the SDLP. While her speeches were often inflammatory, Hume's were more likely to be conciliatory. The small non-sectarian parties, the Ulster Liberals, the NILP and Alliance, avoided taking positions on police order issues for the most part, and when they did took non-controversial positions. For example, the Ulster Liberals appealed to both sides for support for the Public Order Act of 1970, and Alliance in 1972 called on all citizens to work for the restoration of the rule of law. It is difficult to be a moderate in extreme times.

Historically, British parties avoided involvement in Ulster politics, and this hands-off policy was reinforced by the difficulty of finding a solution to the clash of national identities and the resulting violence. When the troubles began, Labour was in power and Callaghan (the Home Secretary) pressed the Unionist government to make reforms in the belief that this would remove the causes of Catholic unrest. As violence escalated, the Labour government sent troops in 1969 and reluctantly took control of the Royal Ulster Constabulary. These policies received bipartisan support from the Conservatives, despite the fact that the Unionist party was affiliated with them at the Westminster level.

Bipartisanship remained in effect after the 1970 election which returned the Conservatives to power. Despite misgivings over internment, Labour did not force a vote in the House of Commons, and Heath invited Wilson and Callaghan to discuss their criticisms of interrogation procedures. Following the meeting, an official inquiry was ordered by Heath.

Bipartisanship faltered after 1971 when Labour politicians began to make statements in favor of a united Ireland. Labour opposition to Conservative security policies was linked to several factors. First, there was the question of civil liberties, with Labour being more sensitive to such issues as censorship of the BBC and internment. As early as 1971 Labour was criticizing the Conservatives for relying too much on military solutions, and ignoring the social roots of the violence. Second, there was a tendency for Labour MPs to sympathize with the Catholics, both because they saw Northern Ireland as a colonial issue, and because many of them were of Irish-Catholic descent or represented constituencies with large numbers of Irish-Catholic voters. The Conservatives in turn were criticized by Labour for a bias towards the Protestants. In September 1971 Wilson warned Heath against allowing 'factional policies' to be imposed by the Ulster government, and said that British policy was no longer neutral in the conflict but allied with the Protestants.

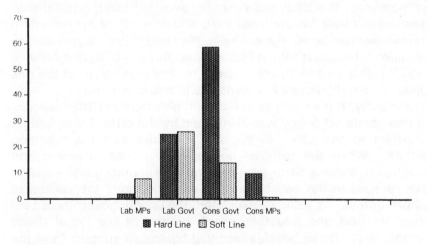

Figure 5.8 Party Attitudes To Public Order in Britain

Labour antagonism towards the Protestants was very clear during the Ulster Workers Council strike in 1974. Wilson called the strike 'sectarian' and 'something out of the seventeenth century', and in a notorious television speech talked of 'bullies and thugs' who had been 'sponging off the British taxpayers'. A third factor determining Labour attitudes was the growing desire among the British public to be rid of the peacekeeping burden. in 1974 the 'Troops Out Movement' was set up to campaign for British withdrawal. The organization supported by various left-wing organizations included six Labour MPs among its sponsors.

Despite these factors, there were other forces which served to maintain a degree of bipartisanship between the Labour and Conservative leadership. Since each party took responsibility for dealing with Ulster in turn (Labour in 1968-70 and 1974-79 the Conservatives for the rest of the time), the realities of the situation produced a convergence in party policies. Both Conservative and Labour ministers were aware of the dangers of communal violence breaking out. Rees, the Labour minister in charge of Northern Ireland warned in 1974 that a British withdrawal would lead to a 'large-scale bloodbath', and communal strife in other parts of the United Kingdom. Also attacks by the IRA on targets in Great Britain and public sympathy for the British troops made it dangerous for left-wing politicians to criticize the army or to support the IRA. This can be seen by the public outrage when the Labour leader of the Greater London Council, Ken Livingstone, invited IRA leaders 'to discuss ways of bringing about a British withdrawal and the reunification of Ireland'. The invitation was severely criticized not only by the Conservatives but also by the Labour Party leader, Michael Foot, who publicly repudiated the invitation and expressed opposition to 'the barbarous methods of the IRA' (*Keesings,* December 1983).

Notes

1. Differences in the electoral systems account for much of this variation. Thus the requirement that parties get 5% of the vote before receiving any representation accounts for the absence of small parties in Germany. In Spain ethnic identities are so strong that small regionally-based parties can get elected. The multiplicity of parties in Spain is also explained by that country's recent emergence from dictatorship, and fewer parties contested the later elections (54 lists in 1979 and only 28 in 1982).

2. For example, in the referendum on the Cossiga laws, the DC, PCI, PSI, PSDI, PRI and PLI campaigned in favor, while the MSI, PR, DP and PDUP campaigned for their abolition.

3. At SDP party conferences there were frequent votes against 'berufsverbot' (the policy of denying government jobs to radicals) and a handful of SDP legislators voted against their own governments anti-terrorist bills.

4. The National Democrats were a nationalist faction composed of professional, university educated Catholics - an early version of the SDLP.

5. For example, a speech calling for a united Ireland would not be included, but one which threatened violence if the British did not agree to a united Ireland would be.

6. It is also, of course, an issue in the Irish Republic, but since no elected representatives of the people of Northern Ireland sit in the Irish legislature, I don't consider this topic.

7. IRA prisoners went on hunger strike for political prisoner status in 1981 and several starved to death, including Bobby Sands who was elected MP for the Fermanagh and South Tyrone constituency.

6 The Electoral Consequences of Political Violence

Who benefits and why?

One reason why politicians criticize one another and articulate certain kinds of policies is because they hope to gain electoral advantage. In this chapter the electoral consequences of political violence will be discussed.[1] Budge and Farlie (1983) argue that law and order issues benefit bourgeois rather than socialist parties, conservatives rather than liberals. This assumption seems plausible in the case of Britain, but does it hold true generally?

Presumably if conservatives benefit from these issues, it is because they are viewed as the best parties for dealing with such matters. Fortunately data are available on public perceptions of the best party on law and order issues for three countries. Table 1 shows that there is a tendency for conservative parties to be seen as the most competent. However, their advantage is neither as consistent nor as strong, as Budge and Farlie suggest. Parties of the Left are sometimes seen as more competent and usually the difference between Left and Right is small. Given that there is nothing intrinsically advantageous to the conservatives in law and order issues, how can these public evaluations be explained? Three factors might predict public attitudes; party policy differences, the level of violence, and the source of the violence.

The public may prefer one party over another because they approve of their policies. Budge and Farlie's conclusion seems to be based upon the following implicit syllogism. The public favors hard-line policies against terrorism. Conservative parties are more likely to advocate hard-line policies. Therefore, the public will view conservative parties as the best on law and order.

Table 6.1
Best Party and Party Advantage on Law and Order Issue

		Right				Left		Conservative Advantage
Germany		CDU	FDP			SDP		+14.4
1976		58.2	8.0			33.8		-1.0
1972		45.9	7.2			46.9		+0.1
1969		48.4	3.3			48.3		
Spain	AP	UCD				PSOE	PCE	
1977	6.9	13.0				14.0	5.0	0.0
1979	3.0	9.7				11.9	2.6	-1.8
		"Right"				"Left"		
1980		27				26		+1.0
Italy	MSI	PLI	DC	PRI	PSDI	PSI	PCI	
1973	11.0	2.7	55.4	2.0	1.2	7.5	20.2	40.2

Sources: Kaase (1978) Reis (1978) Esteban (1979) Maravell (1982) Sani (1975)

As shown earlier, conservative parties do advocate a more hardline set of policies than liberals or leftists, but the difference is not substantial. Election studies usually note that party policies are quite similar, and that there is, therefore, little electoral advantage to the Right. In the 1972 Italian election, for example, all parties 'laid considerable emphasis on law and order without being very definite about the means of achieving it' (Clark and Irving, 1972, p. 214). In Germany in the 1969 election according to Hartman (1970, p. 586) 'the CDU failed to gain from its law and order manifestos. While the Christian Democrats successfully achieved the image of "guardians of public safety" - no mean feat since the SPD rarely showed lack of concern and, in fact, invented some autocratic proposals of its own, to wit, preventive detention - the electorate on the whole did not rise to this bait'. In subsequent elections, they were no more successful, and Irving and Paterson comment with regard to the 1980 election that 'Christian Democratic suggestions that the SPD was...soft on terrorism (did not) carry much weight' (1981, pp. 195-6). They conclude that 'Law and order was not a "non-issue" in 1980 but, as with most of the other issues raised during the campaign, it seemed unlikely to lead to any major transfer of votes' (1981, p. 195-6).

The public might be unaware of specific party positions, and judge governments in terms of results. Governments which preside over a deteriorating security situation will be blamed, while if the level of violence falls, they will receive credit for the outcome. In addition to these overall trends, spectacular triumphs and disasters affect public perceptions. If the authorities capture a terrorist leader or foil a terrorist attack, they will be rated as competent, but if a rescue attempt is botched, they will be seen as ineffective.

Given the variety of criteria that can be used, it is hard to measure government competence with any assurance. In Italy, the steady increase in the level of violence throughout the 'seventies should have harmed the governing DC party, but most accounts suggest that they were not affected. On the other hand the rescue of Dozier, the capture of many terrorists and the consequent decline in violent incidents in 1982, is supposed to have rebounded to the credit of the PRI government in the 1983 elections (Penniman, 1987, p. 106).

In Germany the number of terrorist attacks fell in 1972, and this together with the capture of most of the Baader Meinhof group just prior to the election, made it difficult to criticize the competence of the SDP/FDP coalition. The successful handling of the 1975 Stockholm affair made a strong impression on the public, and presumably helped in the 1976 election. Thereafter violence soared, with 1977 being marked by the Schleyer kidnapping and the Lufthansa hijacking. The latter was resolved by a dramatic and successful commando operation. Chancellor Schmidt 'was almost the exclusive beneficiary in terms of popularity of the widespread sense of public relief that flowed from the Mogadishu success' (Lodge 1981). By 1980 left wing terrorism was no longer a serious threat, and the government and security services were thought to have the problem well in hand, the number of 'most wanted' suspects having been reduced from forty to less than a dozen within three years (Irving and Patterson, 1981, p. 201). Presumably, therefore, the coalition should have gained at every election.

Parties will suffer if they are seen as ideologically similar to those engaging in violence. Thus public attitudes will vary according to whether the threat to public order comes from the extreme Left or the extreme Right. Parties of the Left will be harmed by ultra-leftist violence, those of the Right by ultra-rightist violence. Obviously this will be accentuated or diminished by the ability of politicians to distance themselves from 'their' extremists, and to link opponents to 'their' extremists.

The most important effects apparently result from public perceptions that certain political parties are linked to extremism and violence. In Italy this has harmed both the MSI and the PCI, and consequently benefited the DC. In 1972, the DC was 'helped by the neo-fascist threat and by extremism generally...Andreotti and Fanfani played skillfully on the alarm created by these right and leftwing plots' (Clark and Irving, 1972, p. 219). In 1976, they followed the same strategy arguing that 'the continuing threat of right and left extremism required a stronger center' (Penniman, 1977, p. 137). The electoral hopes of the MSI were destroyed when one of their deputies, Saccucci, was involved in a shooting death at a political rally in 1976. According to Penniman (1977, p. 237) 'In one blow, the incident neutralized all that the MSI-DN had done to present a respectable image and to convince the public that the new right-wing party had excluded hotheads and outright Nazi-Fascists'.

The effect of leftwing violence on the PCI is more difficult to assess. In 1972, Sani argues that the electorate perceived 'the PCI as heavily involved in the strife, or at least unable to restrain its own rank and file from participating in confrontations with the right wing extremists and the police' (Blackmer and Tarrow, 1975, p. 485), and cites a poll showing that 58% thought the Communists were involved in political violence. (This compares with 86% blaming the neo-fascists). However, their strong stand against violence appears to have changed public perceptions by the time of the 1976 election.

'The political effects of the terrorism were important.... The Communist drive for respectability was strengthened. They denounced violence - including Leftwing violence very firmly. Thus the general fear of increasing lawlessness...enhanced the credibility of the Communists' (Clark and Irving, 1977, p. 11). However, the events of the next few years in which leftwing terrorists played the major role, 'forced the PCI on the defensive by establishing in public

opinion a parallelism between terrorists who called themselves
'Communists' and the 'Communism' of the PCI' (Sasson, 1981, p.
229). Thus in the 1979 election both the ultra Left NSU and the PCI
were damaged electorally.[2] 'The Communists, however strongly
they attacked the Red Brigades were hurt by this new instance of
terrorism of the left' (Penniman, 1981, p. 91). By the time of the
1983 election, fears of rightwing terrorism had been renewed, due
to the bombing of the Bologna railway station, so presumably the
MSI rather than the PCI would have suffered.

In Germany, the threats to public order in 1969 and 1972 came
from both the neo-Nazis and the ultra-left so both parties were
equally affected. However, in 1976, despite their tough law and
order stand, the SPD suffered because of the activities of the
Baader-Meinhof group. 'The Angst produced by these law and order
problems tends to benefit the Christian Democrats because some of
the statements made by SDP leftwingers suggest that the SDP still
harbors extremists, or at least people who are sympathetic to
extremists' (Irving and Paterson, 1977, p. 212). By 1980 'The main
threat was still perceived to come from the left', but the threat from
the neo-Nazis 'was demonstrated dramatically and lethally by the
bomb which exploded at the Munich beer festival...killing thirteen
people and injuring over 200' (Irving and Patterson, 1981, p. 201).

Calculating the electoral consequences

There are several ways to calculate the electoral impact of political
violence. We can examine election results to see if there are any
obvious trends, and to compare the expert judgements (cited in the
previous section) to the electoral outcomes. Table 2 shows the
share of the vote going to each ideological bloc of parties in Italy,
Germany and Spain throughout the period.

In Italy and Germany, the vote shows a remarkable stability with
no obvious tendency for the Right to gain at the expense of the Left
or vice versa. Even in those elections where it is claimed that one
party gained from the issue, the vote does not change as one might
expect. For example, in the German election of 1980, the SDP
government could point to its success in capturing most of the
wanted RAF terrorists, and to its spectacular success at Mogadishu
when the hijacked Lufthansa plane was stormed by a commando

team. Yet their share of the vote was virtually unchanged. In Italy in 1983, the governing center-right coalition could claim a similar success against the Red Brigades in the aftermath of the rescue of General Dozier - but their vote fell slightly.

One would expect electoral losses by extremist parties, which are seen by the public as linked to those who engage in violence. There is some evidence that this occurred in Germany where both the extreme Right and the extreme Left declined throughout the period. In Italy, however, the MSI maintained a fairly constant share of the vote, and even showed an increase in 1972 when, according to surveys, the public blamed them for neo-fascist violence! The extreme Left constituted a trivial fraction of the electorate and were fragmented into a number of highly antagonistic groups, but their share of the vote jumped in 1979 - following a period when leftwing violence was at its peak.

Table 6.2
Vote by Ideological Bloc in Italy, Germany and Spain (%)

Italy	1968	1972	1976	1979	1983
Extreme Left	-	1.5	1.5	2.2	1.5
Moderate Left	45.8	41.9	48.5	47.4	47.6
Center Right	46.9	45.6	43.1	43.2	41.4
Extreme Right	5.7	8.7	6.1	5.9	6.8

Germany	1969	1972	1976	1980	
Extreme Left	0.6	0.3	0.4	0.2	
Moderate Left	42.7	45.8	42.6	42.9	
Center	5.8	8.4	7.9	10.6	
Right	46.1	44.9	48.6	44.5	
Extreme Right	4.3	0.6	0.3	0.2	

Spain	1977	1979	1982		
Extreme Left	11.3	12.9	4.1		
Moderate Left	33.7	29.9	48.4		
Center	37.0	34.3	9.6		
Right	8.3	5.8	26.5		
Extreme Right	0.8	2.3	0.6		

Does all this mean that political violence and public order are not important issues to the general public? This seems most unlikely. Budge and Farlie (1983, p. 49) argue that the public is acutely sensitive to political violence and crime. When a breakdown of public order is threatened 'more citizens are likely to feel more affected personally than by any other type of issue - even when it exists as threat rather than actuality'.

However, the extent to which public order issues affect voting would seem to depend upon two factors: the salience of the issue and the degree to which one party is seen as better at dealing with the problem. In Germany in 1976, 7.6% thought public order was the most important issue facing the country. In Italy in 1979, the figure was 10.9%. Let us assume that all these voters cast their votes for the party they thought best at dealing with this problem (See Table 1). Many will, however, end up voting for the same party they would have voted for in the first place.

Where party loyalties are strong, as in Germany and Italy, most voters will consider 'their' party best at solving most problems. However, it is clear there will still be a gain to the CDU and DC since their 'normal' vote is smaller (see Budge and Farlie, 1983). The vote swings are calculated as follows. Issue salience X (Best Party - Normal Vote) = Net Change. This equation produces the following results for the two elections for which we have data.

$$CDU = 0.076 \times (0.582 - 0.469) = +0.9\%$$
$$SDP = 0.076 \times (0.338 - 0.436) = -0.7\%$$
$$PCI = 0.109 \times (0.202 - 0.201) = +0.01\%$$
$$DC = 0.109 \times (0.554 - 0.359) = +2.1\%$$

For other Italian elections, the salience was higher, but for Germany, public concern was probably at its peak in 1976. In neither country does the issue have as much electoral importance as in Spain, Uruguay or Northern Ireland.

Public order and realignment in the Spanish election of 1982

In Spain, no party seems to receive any clear advantage from the issue in the 1977 and 1979 elections. Only a minority of voters see any party as being more competent, and their preferences are distributed in proportion to the general distribution of party identification. However, the dramatic shift in the vote between 1979 and 1982, which resulted in a virtual realignment of Spanish politics, is largely explained by the perceived threat to public order.

There were two distinct movements.

First, the inability of the UCD government to control ETA terrorism led many of its supporters to switch to the hardline AP. Sixty two per cent of those who switched from UCD to AP said that it was because 'terrorism and insecurity were increasing' (Penniman, 1985, p. 312). Second, public order issues led leftwing Spaniards to support the moderate democratic PSOE. Penniman (1985, p. 301) notes 'that fear of violence, military rule, and eventual civil war was very important in mobilizing young voters and former nonvoters on the left. The coup attempt in February 1981 stirred the fear of violence and possible civil war.... military unrest and court-martials did not keep the Spanish people from showing their rejection of military rule. In February 1981 massive demonstrations, larger than any in history, took place in Madrid'.

Alienation in Uruguay

The electoral consequences of political violence in Uruguay are not easy to measure because of the country's unique system of voting. Presidential candidates run under a party label and also under their own 'lema'. Each party is credited with the vote of all candidates on its ticket and the leading candidate of the winning party is elected president. Thus, the total vote for each party is really an aggregate of several distinct factions, and it is necessary to know what each faction represents. Fortunately by 1971, public order had become the dominant issue in Uruguayan politics, so the position of each candidate was well-known.

Ferreira Aldunate's campaign emphasized his total rejection of Pacheco's policies and his opposition to emergency powers. Colorado candidate, Vasconcellos, was also highly critical. Bordaberry, as the hand-picked successor of Pacheco, naturally supported the government's hardline strategy, while General Aguerrondo, a right wing Blanco who had been in charge of Montevideo's police, was clearly identified with a policy of military repression. The fifth candidate, Battle, had on the whole supported Pacheco, but after 1970 had attempted to disassociate himself from the governments unpopular authoritarian policies.

If we consider the 1971 election as a plebiscite on Pacheco's policies, it appears that 36.5% supported him (and might have supported even more repressive policies), 14.6% supported him with some reservation and 47.6% were strongly opposed. Since many of the same politicians ran in 1966, we can compare the two elections to see how political sentiment shifted.

Table 6.3.
Uruguayan Election Results Classified by Candidates Positions (%)

Whole Country	1966			1971
Presidential List [a]	21.3			22.8
Aguerrondo	-	79	51	13.7
Conditional Supporters[b]	57.8			14.6
Liberal Critics[c]	10.2			29.4
Leftist Parties[d]	9.6			18.2
Montevideo				
Presidential Critics	21.3			23.2
Aguerrondo	-	69	41	5.4
Conditional Supporters	47.5			12.6
Liberal Critics	13.7			27.4
Leftist Parties	16.0			30.1

[a] Gestido and Pacheco in 1966, Bordaberry in 1971.
[b] Echegoyan, Gallinal, Heber and Battle in 1966, Battle in 1971.
[c] Michelini and Vasconcellos in 1966, Vasconcellos and Aldunate in 1971.
[d] Communists, Socialists and Christian democrats in 1966, Frente Ampllio in 1971

Source: Fabregat (1972). Figures do not sum to 100% because of minor lists.

In 1966, left/liberal factions received only 19.8% of the vote while the Gestido/Pacheco ticket and the conservative Blancos got 79.1%. It would appear, therefore, that five years of increasingly authoritarian rule and heavy-handed security force tactics had alienated many voters. The law and order position had little electoral appeal for two reasons. First, most Uruguayans were not personally threatened by the Tupamaro attacks, which were carefully targeted against the elite. Second, many were angered by house searches and the loss of their civil liberties. This interpretation is supported by the fact that the vote against hard-line candidates was most apparent in Montevideo, where the security measures impinged most harshly on the population. The most striking change between the two elections was the increased support for the left-wing parties. The Socialist and Communist parties which had traditionally polled around 10% of the total, merged with several other minor parties to form the Frente Amplio or Broad Front) which got 18.2% of the vote in 1971. However, the Frente Amplio was certainly not an extreme left wing party. Although some groups within the coalition were revolutionaries its ideology and programme was moderate and left-of-centre.[3]

Polarization in Northern Ireland

Since the level of political violence and the level of public concern are highest in Northern Ireland, one would expect the greatest effects in that country. However, as Protestants and Catholics have very different attitudes to public order, the political effects are likely to be very different in each community. Subsequent to the outbreak of violence in 1968, the Northern Irish people have been able to express their political sentiments in five local elections, in six elections to the Westminster parliament, and in three elections to a Northern Ireland level assembly. The different types of elections are not completely comparable, so in Table 4 only those for a Northern Ireland parliament are shown. The vote for each party is shown as a percentage of those eligible to vote.

Northern Irish parties can be classified along two dimensions, their position on the constitutional/national question, and their attitudes towards political violence. On the nationalist side, the SDLP supports a united Ireland, but accepts that this can only come about with majority consent, and rejects violence. Sinn Fein on the other hand supports the IRA.[4] In the 1982 election Sinn Fein accused the SDLP of 'compromising and collaborating with British institutions in Ireland', while Hume the SDLP) leader argued that

One of the major issues in this election is that of violence. For the first time in an election the electorate is given a clear opportunity to express its opposition to the campaign of violence which has disfigured our community. The SDLP has candidates in every constituency in order to maximize the turnout throughout the North in a solid rejection of the men of violence.

Table 6.4
Election Results in Northern Ireland (1973-82)

	1973	1975	1982
DUP	7.8	9.5	13.9
OUP	21.1	16.5	18.9
Other Unionists[a]	15.7	13.7	-
NILP/Alliance	8.6	7.2	5.6
SDLP	15.9	15.2	11.3
Worker's Party	1.3	1.4	1.6
Other Nationalists[b]	1.0	-	6.1

Calculated as percentage of eligible voters.
[a]Includes 4.9% for UPNI in 1975.
[b]Republican labour and Nationalists in 1973, PSF in 1982.

The Workers Party advocates a united Socialist Ireland, and rejects IRA violence as counterproductive because it divided the working class along sectarian lines. On the Unionist side, DUP is more hardline and more willing to advocate direct action than is the OUP. The election statistics reveal a growing polarization in three ways. First, the non-sectarian vote declines significantly. This decline is particularly noticeable in the case of the working class NILP, less so for the middle-class suburban-based Alliance Party. Second, within the unionist bloc, the hardline DUP gains at the expense of the OUP and the OUP responds by adopting more extreme positions. Third, on the nationalist side, a similar shift from moderate to militant is shown by the Sinn Fein vote in 1982. Since Sinn Fein did not stand in previous elections, their 1982 vote is sometimes seen as composed of militant republicans who had not voted before. However, an examination of the voting changes for each constituency shows a strong correlation between the number who voted Sinn Fein and the decline in the SDLP vote, and suggests that more than half of the Sinn Fein vote came from those who had previously voted SDLP.[5]

These trends can be explained by the effects of violence. In response to IRA terrorism, Protestants have become more hardline, and thus more likely to vote for DUP.[6] Among Catholics, security force repression produces growing support for the Sinn Fein.[7] Such voting shifts are greatest for young males and for the working class, who are most likely to experience its effects.[8]

Notes

1. Law and order issues are relatively uncommon. Budge and Farlie's Study of 23 democracies during the 1945-81 period shows that only 4.4% of all election issues fell into this category, and that such issues were salient in only one out of every seven elections. However, since our study focuses on countries suffering from political violence, it is not surprising that public order was an issue in every election in every one of the five countries.
2. According to Penniman (1981, p. 209) the NSU's soft stand on terrorism cost it votes. The NSU lamented that terrorism 'made it more difficult to create a consensus on the far left'. Katz (1980, p. 212) pointing out that the Communist vote dropped from 35% to 26% comments that 'No other explanation was asked or given than the death of Aldo Moro'.
3. The Frente advocated land reform, nationalization of the banks and meat-packing industry and a rescheduling of the international debt. Ferreira Aldunate also advocated bank nationalization and land reform. However, Frente Amplio voters had a much more positive image of the Tupamaros as 'well-intentioned revolutionaries' (69%) than the Blancos (34%) or Colorados (34%).
4. Sinn Fein supporters had a highly favorable view of the IRA with 77% thinking them 'patriots and idealists'. Among SDLP voters the figure was only 39% (Fortnight, July 1982). In the 1982 election, Sinn Fein called for the 'immediate withdrawal of the British Army from our land, the disbanding of the sectarian UDR and RUC and self determination for the Irish people'.
5. The rank order of the Sinn Fein vote by constituency is similar to that of SDLP vote losses. The three constituencies where the SDLP vote declined the least (South Antrim, East Belfast and North Down) are all areas where no Sinn Fein candidates stood, while the greatest SDLP vote declines are found in the two constituencies (Mid Ulster, and Fermanagh and South Tyrone) where the Sinn Fein vote was highest.
6. In a 1982 survey, DUP voters were most likely to say that terrorism was the most serious problem facing Northern Ireland (51% versus 41% for OUP voters). DUP received a much

higher proportion of working class than middle class support (19% vs 8%) while OUP had a higher proportion of middle class votes (32% vs 28%).

7. Sinn Fein's support was four times greater among men than women, and twice as high among those aged 18-34 years, than in those 35 and older.

8. Also it is those areas most affected by violence that show the greatest political polarization as can be seen by comparing the vote in the high violence constituencies to the rest of the province.

7 Policies and Outcomes

The most important results of political violence are themselves political in nature. These consequences - changes in political attitudes, government policies and institutions - vary significantly between the societies. Most analyses of the political changes resulting from violence focus on the negative consequences. Violence is seen as a threat to the practice and institutions of liberal democracy, since it encourages extremism, polarization and government authoritarianism. However, there can be positive consequences such as increased democracy and the introduction of reforms to remedy social injustice.

Towards a security state?

Insofar as most definitions of liberal democracy emphasize the necessity of civil liberties, and since protracted political violence usually provokes the imposition of emergency powers which reduce civil liberties, it is a truism to say that political violence has undemocratic effects. However, there are important differences between societies in how much civil liberties are affected, and how government emergency powers were exercised.

Among the five societies examined, Uruguay suffered the most. From mid 1968 onwards, Pacheco and then Bordaberry relied upon emergency powers to rule, and civil liberties were steadily reduced.

After a 'state of internal war' was declared in March 1971, thousands were arrested and hundreds tortured and killed. Finally, in 1973 the military took power and ruled until 1984. At the other extreme, Italy behaved in a restrained fashion. Emergency legislation was enacted but applied very sparingly. (As of July 1977, just over 700 terrorists suspects were in jail or detention).

In the UK and Spain, nationalist insurgencies resulted in significant deprivations of civil liberties in the affected regions (Northern Ireland and the Basque Provinces). Within these areas, sections of the population endured heavy-handed and often brutal security force repression. In Northern Ireland during the 1972-86 period, 50,000 people - 3% of the population - were arrested. In addition, 1,500 persons were interned without trial, and 339,000 houses were searched. These actions fell most heavily on the Catholic minority (Jennings, 1988, p. 196-7). In the Basque provinces, the number of political prisoners was at its maximum in 1975 when there were 749. The number fell steadily until 1977, but then increased, and has been 400-500 since 1981. The number arrested each month averaged about 80 (Clark, 1984, p. 249-64, 1990, p.44-5).

In Germany the number of terrorists imprisoned was small, but large numbers of radicals were screened and denied government jobs. This 'berufsverbot' policy began in 1972 with the passing of the Extremists Decree. A slightly more liberal version was drafted by the Social Democratic government in 1974, but was superseded by the Constitutional Courts decision of 1975. In its judgment the Constitutional Court ruled that all civil servants, whatever their function, have to prove their 'active loyalty' to the free democratic order. The Justices ruled that the examination must take into account the circumstances of each individual case, but membership in a party with unconstitutional goals may be a relevant criterion.

This decision greatly influenced internal security policy concerning extremists in public service. In SDP-governed Lander, membership of radical parties was one criterion of the examination of loyalty, whereas in CDU-governed states membership in extremist parties as a rule implied the rejection of the candidate (von Beyme, 1985, pp. 210-12). During a two year period almost half a million applicants were screened, 5,678 received negative reports and 328 were rejected for employment.

Political rights, such as free speech and the right of assembly, are often curtailed by the authorities, organizations banned and censorship imposed. In Uruguay six leftist parties were banned, and 41 newspapers closed (11 permanently). In other countries, however, political rights were largely maintained although there is censorship of what the authorities consider terrorist propaganda. Thus, in Northern Ireland and the Basque provinces, Sinn Fein and Herri Batasuna (which are generally regarded as political fronts for the IRA and ETA) are allowed to contest elections and to publish newspapers.

Polarization and extremism

The connection between extremism, political polarization and political violence can be made most easily for Northern Ireland and the Basque provinces. Large numbers of voters do support extreme nationalist parties and in both areas, there is an obvious polarization between political parties over public order issues, with nationalists bitterly hostile to what they see as repression.

In Uruguay, political violence served as a catalyst to bring about a political crisis between the president and the legislature. The resort to rule by decree and a reliance on emergency powers by the executive came about because no political consensus could be reached between the president and the legislature, and between the various Blanco and Colorado factions. However, in Germany, Italy and Spain (outside the Basque provinces) there was general agreement among the main parties as to how to deal with political violence. Partisan disagreements were limited and, for the most part, handled responsibly. Indeed in these countries - at least in Italy and Spain - violence may have strengthened democracy because it led to increased cooperation and solidarity between the democratic parties. By the end of the 1970s, the PCI had shown, through its opposition to the revolutionary terrorism of the Red Brigades, that it was genuinely committed to parliamentary democracy. During the Moro affair, the party was more resistant to making concessions then either the Christian Democrats or the Socialists. In Spain, the emerging post-Franco democratic system was threatened by violence from both the revolutionary Left and the extreme Right. The result was that the main parties (PSOE, UCD and AP) made concessions to one another rather than risk conflict that would produce instability and a military coup.

Democracy and Reform

Violence may force the ruling group to concede democratic rights to those who are excluded from the system or to enact reforms. In Northern Ireland, Catholics were excluded from political power in various ways. In local government elections, the householder franchise excluded almost 20% of the population - a disproportionate number of them Catholics. Of more importance, ward boundaries were sometimes gerrymandered to produce Unionist councils in Catholic majority areas. At the Stormont level, the minority had no representatives in the government, and were relegated to a permanent opposition status.

In response to civil rights demonstrations and communal rioting, London reformed the system to respond to Catholic grievances. The local government franchise was extended to all adults, and a system of proportional voting was introduced for all elections to ensure that all shades of political opinion were fairly represented. The UK government announced that it would not accept any Northern Irish government that did not contain representatives from both communities. Constituency boundaries were redrawn so as to maximize Catholic representation.

Other reforms were made to deal with religious discrimination and unemployment. For example, a Housing Executive was established to allocate public housing fairly, and a massive house building program was started. A parliamentary commissioner was appointed to examine complaints of government discrimination and the Fair Employment Agency set up to monitor employment. In an attempt to improve economic conditions, the government spent vast sums to create new jobs in areas of high unemployment (Boyle, 1980, pp. 9-12). The best-known of these projects was the DeLorean Motor Company which provided 2000 jobs in Catholic areas of West Belfast at a cost of £80 million in government loans and grants.

In the Basque case, the threat of ETA violence was certainly one of the main reasons that the Spanish government granted autonomy to the region and made various other reforms. In November 1975 a decree was issued tolerating regional languages, in December 1978 the constitution declared regional languages co-official with Spanish, and in January 1978 the teaching of the Basque language in the schools was extended. By a series of amnesties in November 1975, July 1976, March 1977, and May 1977 all the Basque political prisoners were given their freedom. Beginning in May 1976, when political associations were allowed, Spain moved steadily towards democracy; the first free elections were held in June 1977 and the new constitution came into effect on December 28, 1978. Discussions on Basque autonomy began in September 1977, the autonomy statue was formulated in July 1979, approved by a referendum in the Basque provinces in October 1979, and finally, in March 1980, elections were held for a Basque parliament.

In the case of Italy, according to Tarrow (1989), popular disturbances resulted in increased mobilization and participation. He argues that 'Italy developed a broader repertoire of participation than it possessed when the cycle began. If strikers were more likely to use violence by its end, they were also more likely to organize marches and public meetings, to use assemblies to plan their demands, and to form grassroots bodies. In a number of other sectors, new institutions and practices developed, reversing the disruptiveness of the early phase of the cycle but also providing social actors with resources to advance their goals. Institutional expansion of participation accompanied violence as mobilization declined' (Tarrow, 1989, p. 311). At the end of the decade, Italian political culture had changed fundamentally. Women, students and other groups who had been treated as wards by the organizations and political parties that claimed to represent them, rejected this paternalism and demanded autonomy. New social actors emerged as previously quiescent groups demanded a place in the political process, and forced new issues onto the agenda.

Three patterns of consequences

If the outcomes of political violence are considered from the perspectives of both the insurgents and the regime, three patterns can be distinguished. These appear to describe not only the cases that have been examined, but also the experience of other societies threatened by political violence.

Resilient democracies

For some societies the outcome of political violence can be characterized by what does not happen. The democratic status quo is resilient, and its constitutional forms and institutions remain intact. The insurgents fail almost totally in their objectives. Political polarization is moderate. Emergency powers are exercised in a restrained fashion. This description would seem to apply to Italy, Spain (outside the Basque Provinces) and Germany.

Two Latin American democracies, Venezuela and Columbia, also fall into this group. Despite having to face an armed insurrection in 1963, and terrorist attacks throughout the 1970s, Venezuela is regarded as one of the most stable democracies in the region with a good human rights record.[1] Two moderate parties, the social democratic AD and the Christian Democratic COPEI dominate electoral politics; the Marxist left vote in the 1988 presidential elections was only 3%. Similarly Columbia, despite chronic violence involving leftist guerrillas, urban terrorism, right wing death squads and widespread 'narco-terrorism' has maintained a stable two-party democratic system with freedom of the press and honest elections (Peeler, 1985, p. 112-3). Although large numbers have been detained without trial, and there have been occasional human rights violations, government policy has emphasized amnesty and legalization of the extreme left. This finally resulted in an agreement whereby the guerrillas laid down their arms and were granted a role in a constitutional convention. In the presidential elections of 1986, their Union Patriotica candidate received only 4.5% of the vote.

Regimes overthrown by military coups

In the cases we examined, only in Uruguay was democracy overthrown and replaced by a military dictatorship. However, this outcome is found in several other cases, such as Argentina, Chile and Turkey. Here the insurgents can be said to have had at least a negative success. Their violence created a political crisis, and severe political polarization. The crisis was 'resolved' the same way in all four countries - by a military take-over followed by savage repression. Regis Debray's comment that 'the gravediggers of liberal Uruguay also dug their own graves' applies to other countries as well. Not only the revolutionary insurgents but many merely suspected of sympathizing with them suffered during this reaction. In Argentina, at least 10,000 'disappeared after being tortured and interrogated by the military, and hundreds were murdered by rightist death squads. In Turkey, militants of both right and left as well as trade union and student activists were rounded up. Altogether more than 40,000 were arrested in the weeks after the coup, and two years later 10,000 remained in custody, many without having been formally charged. More than 600 were tried for committing and abetting terrorism, and some were hanged. In Chile, the level of repression following the 1973 coup was unprecedented. Estimates placed the number of leftists killed at between 3,000 and 11,000. Between 40,000 and 95,000 were imprisoned. Thousands were dismissed from their jobs for political reasons; and thousands fled into exile. The state of siege, involving censorship, curfews, detention without trial and the banning of political organizations was gradually relaxed, but remained in effect until 1982.

These military regimes lasted for several years, in Uruguay from 1973-84, in Argentina from 1976-83, in Chile from 1973-89 and in Turkey from 1980-83. Since one revolutionary strategy argues that repression will result in polarization and radicalization, it is instructive to compare the electoral results before and after the military regimes. An examination of the statistics shows that the electorate became more moderate in Chile and Argentina. In the December 1989 elections in Chile, the Christian Democratic candidate won the presidency with an outright majority (54%), while in the legislature the Socialist Parties fell from 42% to 28% of the total. In Argentina, the Peronist share of the vote fell from 62% to 40%, while the middle-of-the-road Civil Radical Union became the majority party, increasing its vote from 23% to 52%.

In Turkey, although the military banned the old parties, 'the 1983 election revealed a continuity of basic political alignments. Since the beginning of the multiparty era in 1950, right and center parties have received approximately two-thirds of the votes cast in national elections. In November 1983 over 68 percent of the electorate voted for either the MP or the NDP' (Pitman, 1988, p. 253). There was similar continuity in Uruguay, with each party's 1984 vote being very similar to that of 1971. The Frente Amplio, for example, got 18.2% in 1971 and 20.4% in 1984.

There is, I think, a clear conclusion to be drawn from the evidence. Violence is not an effective strategy for bringing about a socialist revolution in contemporary capitalist democracies. Revolutionary terrorism has failed to generate a revolutionary situation in any of the countries that we examined. This is true both in the short-run and in the long-run, and despite the fact that revolutionaries have employed a variety of sophisticated tactics.

The failure of the revolutionaries, however, has taken two forms. First, in the resilient democracies, political revolutionaries and their supporters are such a small group that they pose no significant threat. The lives of ordinary citizens are not significantly affected by political violence nor government security policies. The public supports the government and security forces in their actions against the revolutionaries. This was the case not only in Italy and Germany, but also in Venezuela and Colombia. According to Peeler (1985, p. 125)

If dissidents choose - or are forced into - insurgency against a functioning liberal democratic system, they are likely to find themselves morally and politically isolated and militarily vulnerable. The insurgents have the unenviable task of convincing people that the government for which they voted is not really their government, that, on the contrary, this group of self-appointed rebels is the legitimate government. In such a situation repressive measures often have popular support. The Venezuelan governments of Betancourt and Leoni (AD) repressed the insurgents of the 1960s quite severely, leaving them receptive to the amnesty and legalization offered by Caldera after 1969. A similar situation seems to be evolving in Colombia now.

Given the limited appeal of revolutionary ideologies, government repression is both mild and selective. The institutions of liberal democracy are maintained.

In the second group of countries, democracy was overthrown by the military. The question therefore, is to explain why this happened. The common element in all four cases is that the military perceived a threat to themselves and the social order. Although the specifics vary between countries, certain common factors are apparent.

It is clear that popular support for radical change and extremism was much stronger as can be seen by both voting statistics and public opinion polls. Whereas revolutionary leftist parties in the resilient democracies received under 5%, in Uruguay the Frente Amplio got 18.2% of the vote, and in Chile, Allendes' Popular Unity coalition obtained 43.4%. In Argentina, since the Peronist movement included both revolutionary socialists and conservative authoritarians, it is difficult to use voting statistics as an indicator.[2] However a 1971 survey revealed that 48% of Argentineans thought 'armed struggle justifiable' - a figure even higher than the proportion of Uruguayans (39%) who thought the Tupamaros 'well-intentioned revolutionaries'. In Turkey, although Marxist parties have never been more than a marginal factor in national politics,[3] there was significant and growing support for the ultra-rightist Nationalist Action Party, and for the Muslim fundamentalist National Salvation Party. In the 1977 elections, these two parties polled 15% of the vote.

The threat posed by political extremism took three forms. First, there was the threat to the established social order. One common interpretation of the Chilean coup is that the military intervened to prevent Allende's government from carrying out a socialist transformation though democratic means. Similarly in Uruguay, not only the Frente Amplio but other politicians advocated extensive nationalization and land redistribution. This view of the army as playing a counterrevolutionary role can be supported by the fact that in Chile and Argentina, the privileged strata welcomed the military take-overs.[4] In Turkey, however, the threat was not against capitalism but to the secular principles of Kemalism.

> The NSP sponsored a massive rally at Konya, where religious fundamentalists demonstrated to demand the reinstatement of Islamic law in Turkey, reportedly showing disrespect for the flag and the national anthem. These acts were regarded as an open renunciation of Kemalism and a direct challenge to the military. On September 7, therefore, General Evren met secretly with armed forces and police commanders to set in motion plans for another coup (Pitman, 1988, p. 81).

Second, extremist violence led to a breakdown of public order which posed a threat to the general public. In Turkey, as many as 2000 died in fighting between leftists and rightists in the two years before the coup. In Chile the center of Santiago became a battlefield of right and left wing activists. Many ordinary citizens welcomed the military takeover as the only alternative to anarchy.[5]

Third, the military intervened because they were directly threatened by political violence. The involvement of the Uruguayan military in the anti-Tupamaro campaign began after the assassination of 'four alleged leaders of an extreme right-wing anti-Tupamaro group. Among the victims was a navy captain, who became the first armed forces officer killed by the Tupamaros. In response the military demanded the declaration of internal war, under which the armed forces were set free to pursue their counterinsurgency objectives' (Porzecanski, 1973, p. 68).

In Chile, Moss claims that the coup was provoked by 'the efforts of the extreme left to incite rebellion within the armed forces themselves. This last factor, was what finally tipped the balance. The armed forces had to move in September, not only to save the country but to save themselves' (Moss, 1973, p.ii).

In all four countries, the inability of the civilian governments to maintain public order was linked to other weaknesses. In every case, the economy was in severe crisis with rampant inflation, high unemployment and industrial unrest. There was extreme political polarization between the President and the legislature in both Chile and Uruguay. Indeed in Chile, the Chamber of Deputies approved by 81 votes to 47, a motion of censure against the government for having violated the constitution, which appealed to the armed forces to 'reestablish the constitution and the law' (Keesings, 1973, p. 26149).

In Turkey, no party had a majority in the national Assembly which was therefore unable to fulfil its constitutional responsibility to elect a President. The work of the government was at a standstill due to the obstructionist tactics of the opposition. In Argentina, after the death of Peron, his wife (and Vice President) succeeded him. Lacking his charisma she relied heavily upon her advisor, Lopez Rega - who supposedly made policy decisions on the basis of astrology. Thus, the military intervened against civilian governments, which had only minority support, and consequently lacked legitimacy.

Chronic ethnic conflict

A third pattern is found in Northern Ireland and the Basque Provinces. In both areas, the level of violence remains high, and even after more than twenty years shows no sign of ending. It is the long-lasting nature of these conflicts which is their most striking feature and which distinguishes them from revolutionary insurgencies.

Not only do ethnic conflicts endure longer, they also have more impact on society. The death rate is usually far higher. In Northern Ireland with a population of 1.5 million there have been almost 3000 killed, while in the Basque provinces with 2.2 million people over 600 have died. In both regions the economic impact of political violence has been devastating, as compared to the relatively trivial effects of revolutionary terrorism in countries such as Italy. Fear of violence leads the public to avoid bad areas, to stay in at night, etc. The counter-insurgency policies adopted by the security forces result in further disruptions of public routines.

Why does ethnic violence affect society more than revolutionary violence? To answer this question, it is necessary to look at the strategy of nationalist insurgency - and at how their campaigns work out in ethnically divided societies. Nationalists see their land as being occupied by foreigners and their goal is to raise the costs to the occupiers. ETA theorists saw the 'victories of the Algerian and Vietnamese revolutions against France...as the correct models' for their own struggle. They believed the Basque provinces were 'suffering from a colonial relationship just as surely as had Algeria or Vietnam under the French' (Clark, 1984, p. 34). For Irish nationalists, the Easter Rebellion of 1916 which ended with the creation of the Irish Free State, and other anticolonial insurgencies provided inspiration (MacStiofain, 1975, p. 41, 70-9). According to McGuire 'The main examples followed by the Provisionals....were the guerilla campaigns against the British in Cyprus in the 1950s and Aden in the 1960s' (1973, p. 78).

Nationalist campaigns are very different, therefore, from those of revolutionary terrorists who carefully target members of the elite.[6] The enemy is defined more broadly. In Northern Ireland, the IRA tries to kill as many soldiers and police as they can, and by bombing economic targets they hoped to 'drive out international investors and make it so costly for the British...that they would have to meet our demands' (McGuire, 1973, p. 78,34). Given the high number of attacks directed against them, the security forces respond with heavy handed repression. This repression falls heavily upon ordinary members of the ethnic community from which the terrorists are drawn. The result is that they become increasingly alienated from the regime.

In a classic colonial situation, such as Aden or Algeria, the nationalist strategy works because the colonial power and the settlers eventually find the costs too great. The colonial power pulls out, the settlers go home. However, the strategy fails in Northern Ireland and the Basque Provinces, because in neither case is the colonial settler-state analogy appropriate. Unlike Algeria or Aden where the population was ethnically distinct from their metropolitan rulers, in Northern Ireland and the Basque Provinces a very large proportion are not members of the nationalist community. In Northern Ireland more than 60% are British Protestants while in the Basque provinces ethnic Spaniards constitute about 40%. Furthermore, even many ethnic Basques and Irish Catholics do not see their situation as one of colonial subordination and exploitation. Basques are integrated into the political and business elite of Spain. Northern Irish Catholics benefit from the British welfare state. Thus 'moderate Basques...assert that complete independence is neither feasible nor desirable...Euzkadi is too small to survive as an independent sovereign state' (Clark, 1984, p. 170-1), and among Northern Irish Catholics only a plurality favor Irish unity. Consequently, in each region nationalists constitute only about 20% of the total population.[7]

This degree of support produces a political and military stalemate. The government is unable to defeat the guerrillas militarily since they have too much support, concentrated within their ethnic community. Both the IRA and ETA can always find recruits and shelter, and therefore keep up their war of attrition. This unremitting low intensity violence has undoubtedly been effective in weakening the resolve of the metropolitan powers. In Britain the general public wants the troops withdrawn and favors Irish unity. The Labour Party is officially committed to a United Ireland, although official British policy, endorsed by all the major parties, is that unity can only come about by majority consent. The Spanish public and political parties are more resistant to nationalist demands than the British. The conservative Partido Popular regards national unity as non-negotiable, although the PSOE is willing to concede a degree of self-determination. It is reasonable to assume that the granting of regional autonomy to the Basque provinces and other concessions were a result of ETA violence.

However, after more than two decades neither the IRA nor ETA has realized their ultimate goal. Why then do they keep on fighting? Why don't they accept that theirs is a minority position? The short answer is that they believe they will become a political majority. A variety of benign scenarios have been suggested by Irish nationalists in which the Protestants will finally recognize their Irish identity.[8] Both the IRA and ETA have in fact received increased electoral support. The Herri Batasuna vote has risen steadily from 1979, and in the 1986 elections to the Basque Parliament they won 17.5 percent. Provisional Sinn Fein's vote went from 64,000 in 1982 to 103,000 in 1983.

A second reason for the guerrillas to keep fighting is psychological. Clark's comments on ETA militants would also apply to the IRA. 'Many of these men, now in their late twenties or early thirties, have been engaged in violent struggle since they were adolescents. They do not know any other way of life....They continue to fight because they do not know what else they can do' (1984, p. 279). Clark also points out that violence can be self-sustaining. 'Wars, and especially civil wars, seem to spawn feuding that persists perhaps for a generation after the main struggle has terminated. The presence of revenge or grudge killings in the ETA record over the past two years suggests that something like this is beginning to occur in the Basque case' (1984, p. 278).

Self-sustaining violence may be particularly characteristic of ethnic conflicts. Violence by nationalists provokes violence by those who are loyal to the system. In Northern Ireland, IRA attacks resulted in loyalist terrorism, and hundreds of Catholic deaths. Several times, the conflict has involved a deadly cycle of tit-for-tat killings, in which each side took reprisals. Some writers (Kuper, 1981, Thompson, 1985) argue that ethnic conflicts have a tendency to become genocidal. Since the militants on each side are clearly identified with a particular ethnic community, it is easy to assume, for example, that all Catholics are aligned with the IRA and therefore legitimate targets for loyalists death squads. Similarly MacStiofain, the head of the IRA, is reputed to have remarked when Protestants were killed as a result of IRA bombings 'What does it matter, they're all bigots anyway' (McGuire, 1973).

Ethnic violence and security force repression serve to polarize divided societies, like the Basque Provinces and Northern Ireland even further. There is sharp cleavage in attitudes towards political violence between Basques and Spaniards, Catholics and Protestants, which reflects the different experiences of each group. Since politicians must represent their followers deeply held opinions, it is difficult for them to negotiate a peaceful resolution of the conflict. Since the conflicts remain unresolved, it is likely that political violence will continue into the foreseeable future.

What can governments do?

It can be argued that the most severe disruptions are produced not by political violence itself but by the governments' response to it. In this final section, the question of what should - and what should not - be done by governments faced with political violence will be discussed. Broadly speaking, government policies for dealing with political violence fall into three types, repressive, reformist, and propagandist.

One of the most important policy choices that governments make concerns the degree to which they deprive their citizens of their civil liberties, and use the security forces to repress them. The first rule should be that such policies be used as little as possible. The obvious result of large-scale indiscriminate use of the army and police to repress political violence is to alienate the general population. This alienation is so intense in Northern Ireland, the Basque provinces and Uruguay that even moderate politicians are forced to take a stand against security policies. The issue of public order dominates the politics of these societies, exacerbates political polarization and makes it difficult for politicians to negotiate the underlying issues and conflicts. Furthermore there is no evidence that these kinds of repressive policies are effective in reducing political violence (Hewitt, 1984).

This does not mean that such measures can never be justified. As a temporary response to a clear emergency, such as widespread disorders (e.g. communal rioting in Ulster) or a terrorist atrocity (e.g. the kidnapping of Aldo Moro), road blocks, curfews and house searches seem appropriate. However, there are dangers in overreacting, and it is easy for emergency measures to become institutionalized as they did in Uruguay and Northern Ireland. In Germany, the government had a very minor problem with the Baader-Meinhof terrorists. Yet, they adopted draconian measures to deal with the situation, and engaged in a witchhunt of their putative sympathizers.

Many writers argue that political violence is due to social injustice and that governments should respond by making reforms so that the grievances of terrorists and rioters are redressed. Writing about Italy, Silj (1979, p. xix-xx) thought that political violence would increase unless there was social justice and...economic and social growth', while Bell (1978, p. 259) argued that 'Italy faces not so much a terrorist problem as a need to restructure its society'. This is a plausible view but there is ambiguity about what reforms are to be made. Should the government respond to the demands made by politically organized groups, or to what experts think are the real problems? For example, the goal of the Red Brigades was the overthrow of capitalism and its replacement by a socialist society. Yet few advocates of reform suggest that such a transformation be carried out, and instead identify a number of specific problems which need to be resolved. Thus both Bell and Silj point to the archaic university system and high rate of unemployment among the young as factors that produce violence.

Nationalist conflicts are more likely to be accepted at face value, although in Northern Ireland British policy makers initially treated the problem as one of religious discrimination and unemployment. Successive British administrations therefore concentrated on these issues. The results have been minimal, and Catholic alienation and political violence remain high. This suggests that the conflict in Northern Ireland is not about civil rights and jobs, but about nationalism. British failure in Northern Ireland implies that one of the first requirements of successful conflict regulation is correctly identifying what the conflict is about.

Nationalist conflicts are particularly difficult to solve. The positions taken often appear irreconcilable, with no compromise possible. Irish nationalists want a Thirty Two County Irish Republic but Ulster Unionists want to remain part of the United Kingdom. Basque nationalists want an independent Euskadi but most of the inhabitants of the region want to remain part of Spain. Opinions are strongly held and since they are linked to ethnic identity change little over time. Concessions to one side anger the other, often leading to a backlash. (For example, the setting up of the Council of Ireland in 1974 provoked massive resistance from the Unionists, and led to the collapse of the power sharing executive).

One sensible strategy for governments faced with this type of situation is to recognize that they are only one of several actors involved, and to facilitate negotiations between them. Clark (1990,

p. 2-3) argues that 'if the rebels are so strongly supported by their host population that the government cannot suppress them.....then negotiations become the only realistic way out of violence. In other words, negotiations may be the best solution to insurgency, not because it is such a good option, but simply because all the others are so bad'.

Successful negotiations must involve all the important organizations and interests involved in the conflict. At a minimum, this will include all the local political parties - both militants and moderates. In Northern Ireland, this means that representatives of Sinn Fein, the SDLP, DUP and OUP would be involved, and in the Basque provinces, Herri Batasuna, Euskadiko Ezkerra, the PNV and the PSOE. In addition to the British government, the Irish Republic must also be included in talks about Northern Ireland.

Based on the Basque case, Clark suggests a number of factors that can affect the negotiations. The agenda should be controlled so as to prevent anti-negotiation elements from sabotaging the talks. Negotiations should be kept out of the public eye, at least initially. The various parties should avoid laying down preconditions at the start of talks - particularly demands that violence stop before talks begin. A two-track negotiation strategy should be used to separate the issues into two categories, political and technical.

Such a division makes it possible for parties in conflict to negotiate with one another without actually appearing to do so. One negotiation arena is set aside for issues that can plausibly be characterized as narrowly technical, and for which institutional mechanisms and procedures already exist. Amnesty for convicted insurgents would be an example of one such issue (Clark, 1990, p. 236).

For negotiations to lead to conflict resolution there must be some outcome that is acceptable to a clear majority of those involved. In the Basque Provinces a movement towards consensus has taken place. Most parties accept Basque autonomy within a federal Spain, and consider the regional institutions legitimate and democratic. The only two parties opposed to this situation are Herri Batasuna, which wants full independence and the Right wing Partido Popular which opposes Basque autonomy. In the most recent elections to the Basque Parliament in 1986, these two parties received 17.5% and

5% of the vote.

In Northern Ireland, there are also indications that a consensus may be emerging. The core principle seems to be the right to self-determination of the people of Northern Ireland. This principle is strongly supported by all the Unionist parties, and accepted by the constitutional nationalists (the SDLP) and the Irish Republic. Since almost all Protestants and a large number of Catholics want to remain within the UK, this means that the constitutional status of Northern Ireland will remain unchanged for the immediate future. Still unresolved, however, are Irish nationalist demands for a guaranteed role in any local legislature and for an 'Irish dimension' in Northern Irish politics.

One important aspect of violent conflicts involves a struggle between the government and the dissidents to influence public opinion. Governments sometimes attempt to counter terrorist propaganda by censorship. In Uruguay the press was forbidden to use the word 'Tupamaro' and prohibited from publishing any news of guerrilla activity, except that supplied by the government. In Spain, a 1984 law makes it a criminal offense to support or praise 'the activities typical of a terrorist organization...or the deeds or commemorative dates of their members by publishing or broadcasting via the mass media, articles expressing opinions, news reports, graphical illustrations, communiques, or by any other form of dissemination'. Similarly, West Germany in 1976, brought in the Anti-Constitutional Advocacy Act, making it an offense to publicly advocate and/or encourage others to commit an offenses against the stability of the Federal Republic. However, the moral ambiguity of restricting free speech in order to defend democracy is counterproductive and frequently engenders sympathy for the dissidents. Therefore, it is better for the government to refute terrorist arguments by a vigorous public relations campaign. In its own propaganda, the government needs to explain and justify the security policies that it adopts, and to publicize the reforms it has made. At the same time the authorities must not create panic among the general public by exaggerating the dangers posed by political violence.

Violent conflicts can end in several ways. Very rarely insurgents succeed in making a revolution or gaining national independence. In a handful of cases, negotiations have produced a viable settlement. Usually, however, the regime either crushes the dissidents or the political violence gradually subsides, without any substantial reforms being made. This being so, I would suggest that governments should not overreact to political violence, either by adopting unnecessarily harsh policies or by rushing to make sweeping and inappropriate reforms. Western societies and their democratic institutions are resilient, and usually able to tolerate a considerable amount of political violence without serious consequences.

Notes

1.   Amnesty International in a 1989 report accused the Venezuelan army of murdering some fishermen, and of overresponding to urban riots. However, in a regional context, Venezuela and Colombia have relatively benign records. As Peeler (1985, p. 127-8) notes both have 'been characterized by considerably more personal security against political violence than is the norm in Latin America..... Most of their citizens may be expected to see and appreciate the difference. In Latin America today, the government that does not murder large numbers of its citizens is performing relatively well'.

2.   The split in the Peronist movement was so intense that at the rally to welcome Peron's return to Argentina on June 20, 1973 gunfire was exchanged between the different factions leaving several hundred dead and over 1000 injured (Rudolph, 1985, p. 65).

3.   Four Marxist parties contested local elections in 1980, just before the military crackdown, but gathered only 1% of the vote nationwide (Pitman, 1988, p. 352).

4.   The Argentine coup 'was welcomed by the landed and business interests' (Rudolph, 1985, p. 66).

5.   This was especially true in Turkey (Pitman, 1988, p. 81) but also explained public support in Argentina (Rudolph, 1985, p. 66) and Chile (Keesings, 1976, p. 26149).

6.   According to Porzecanski (1973, p. 48) 'Tupamaro tactics...were undertaken with great marksmanship, avoided the use of indiscriminate violence and concentrated on delivering one individual blow after another. An Italian official noted that 'since the Red Brigades normally claim credit for their violent acts with special messages, the singling out of the victim and the personalization of the attack are very important'.

7.   According to the surveys cited by Clark (1984, p. 172) support for independence in the Basque provinces averaged 20% during 1976-82. The high point came in 1979 when 36% favored independence, but since then it has declined. In Northern Ireland, two polls in 1974 and 1985 found a plurality of Catholics for a united Ireland (46% and 47%),

while a significant number (37% and 34%), favored remaining part of the United Kingdom.

8. Holland (1981, p. 202) argues that if the British did withdraw Protestants would accept the situation 'Once the British left, the loyalists would have little to fight for - they could not hope by terrorism to bring the British back. Whatever sense of Ulster nationalism there is among Protestants is not strong enough to lend emotional support or political backing for a loyalist campaign aimed at establishing a Protestant state independent from Ireland'.

Appendix: Data Sources

The data used in the study are discussed under three headings; political violence and security force countermeasures, economic conditions, and public opinion polls.

Political violence and security force countermeasures

Uruguay

The main source for Tupamaro actions, and security force countermeasures is a 63 page chronology in Spanish by Mayans (1971). Mayans' study is described by one expert on Latin American terrorism as the most complete single volume compilation of documentary materials relating to the Tupamaro movement...the best reference work available today in English or Spanish' (Russell, 1974, p. 73). Mayans usually provides details on victim characteristics, bombing targets, ransoms paid, money stolen in bank robberies, etc. Unfortunately, the chronology only goes up to March 1971 (i.e., to the point at which a state of internal war was declared). For the two year period following, during which the Tupamaros were crushed by the army, the sources are Litt and Kohl's chronology (1974) which runs from June 1962 through July 1973 and a report by the Uruguayan Ministry of the Interior covering seven months in 1972.

How well these sources report Tupamaro violence and government countermeasures is difficult to assess, since the government exercised censorship over press reports of the conflict. One figure is known, however, and can be used to estimate the degree of coverage. According to Porzecanski (1973, p. 28), 648 Tupamaros were captured from December 1966 through June 1972, while our count for a slightly shorter period, January 1968 to June 1972, is 606. This suggests that, during this period, our sources record almost all the activity. After the state of internal war was declared on April 15, 1972, the figures are less reliable, although the Interior Ministry report gives statistics on terrorist acts, number of terrorists arrested, weapons found and houses searched for each of the seven months.

Northern Ireland

The fatalities associated with Northern Irish conflict are, for the most part, well-documented. Our death file has been created by combining several sources, cross checking them against one another and, if possible, finding any information still missing. The records kept by the Royal Ulster Constabulary (RUC) are the basic source for Northern Irish fatalities. The RUC records generally give the name, age, address, where a person was killed and the cause of death (i.e., gun shot wounds, explosion, etc.). Unfortunately, the records usually do not provide information on the victim's religion, whether or not the victim was a member of a terrorist organization, or by whom the person was killed. Thus, it is not possible to distinguish between, for example, people shot by the army or those assassinated by terrorists. Fortunately, the files maintained by the Belfast Office of the *Irish Times,* while based upon the RUC files, provide additional information as to the circumstances surrounding a death, the likely killer and the characteristics of the victim. The RUC/Irish Times records do not begin until October, 1971. For deaths prior to this date, there are two sources. *The Belfast Newsletter,* (8 September 1971) lists the first 100 deaths, giving name, age, address and a brief characterization of the cause of death. A written answer to a question in the House of Commons (26 October 1971, pp. 56-70) gives the name, age, occupation, place where killed, date and cause of death for the first 100 victims in 1971.

The British army keeps records on violence and security force counter-measures including monthly statistics on explosions, incidents in which the security forces were fired upon, incidents in which the security forces opened fire, houses searched, weapons found, arrests for terrorist offenses and army force levels. From February 1973 to December 1975, the army recorded a statistic 'terrorists out of action' which refers to the total number interned at the end of each month. Beginning January 1976, when internment was ended, this was replaced by a category 'charges for terrorist offenses'. The 'weapons found' and 'terrorists out of action' categories are broken down by religion. Since the U.K. government provides compensation for both personal injury and property damage, statistics are available on the direct costs of terrorist violence.

Spain

The Spanish authorities do not release detailed information on terrorism nor on counter-insurgency operations. In order to construct a data set, the main sources used were Equipo Cinco (1977), Del Campo (1982) and a chronology covering the 1973-83 decade (Equipo D: 1984). For the period after January 1980, the U.S. Consulate in Bilbao provided information on terrorist incidents in the Basque region, based on local newspaper reports. Professor Robert Clark, George Mason University, has developed a data - set of ETA attacks, which I have used as a check on my data. While Clark has collected more information on woundings and kidnappings, our statistics on ETA killings are fairly similar overall. For the 1975-1980 period, Clark found 250 killings while my sources list 243.

Italy

The Ministry of the Interior provides data on the total number of terrorist incidents. These official statistics include acts of widely varying severity, minor acts of vandalism as well as homicides and kidnappings. Information on serious attacks such as killings, woundings, kidnappings, etc., is given in the Partido Communisti Italiano (Sezione problemi dello Stato), Pisano (1979) and Galleni (1981). The most detailed information is found in the annual and semi-annual reports put out by the PCI. These list those killed and wounded in terrorist attacks and give the name, victim characteristics, date and place of attack and group responsible. A comparison between the PCI data and that from other sources does not reveal any obvious bias or omissions. The PCI statistics also agree closely with the other sources as to the targets of the attacks. The *New York Times, London Times, Keesings,* and *Pisano* (l979) are the sources for terrorist captures and arrests. Figures of the total number of terrorists in jail are given irregularly and are usually broken down by organization (Red Brigade, Front Line, etc.).

West Germany

Several chronologies of terrorism in West Germany exist. The primary source for such chronologies is usually the Federal Criminal Office (Bundeskriminalamt) in Wiesbaden. Althammer (1978) contains a forty page chronology. The most complete listing can be found in A. Jeschke and W. Malanowski (1980). This chronology of almost seventy pages covers domestic left- and right-wing terrorism events as well as foreign events bearing on the German scene for the period 1967-1980. Compiled by the working group 'Oeffentlichkeitsarbeit gegen Terrorismus' of the Ministry of the Interior, it lists attacks on persons and on property as well as armed robberies by various terrorist groups on an annual basis. For each event, the date, location, nature of the act and the group responsible are listed.

Economic conditions

The best single source on economic conditions is the *United Nations Statistical Office Monthly Bulletin of Statistics* which contains information on unemployment, industrial production, etc.   Other statistics can be found in the *Yearbook of International Trade Statistics,* the *Yearbook of National Accounts Statistics,* the *Yearbook of Industrial Statistics* and the *Statistical Yearbook.*
Further economic data on a national or regional basis are obtainable for Northern Ireland, Uruguay and Spain. The Northern Irish statistics up to September 1977 are from the Northern Ireland Department of Finance, Digest of Statistics. For the period since

then the figures are provided by the Department of Manpower Services, Belfast. Uruguay was one of the most economically developed and socially progressive societies in Latin America, and a wealth of information on economic conditions is available in the publications of the Instituto de Estudios Politicos, the Institute de Economia and Banco de la Republica Oriental del Uruguay. *Boletin Estadistico Statistics* on unemployment were supplied privately by the Direccion General de Estadistica y Censos.   The Banco de Espana, *Boletin Estadistico* gives some Spanish monthly economic statistics on a regional basis. Monthly statistics on tourism for most countries can be obtained from the World Tourism Organization, *World Travel Statistics.*

Public opinion

There are two types of public opinion survey; those conducted by academics and those carried out by commercial survey organizations (usually for newspapers or magazines).   I collected, by library research and writing to polling organizations and academics, a large amount of published and unpublished material.

For Uruguay, there is a two volume survey of attitudes towards political violence and the state of emergency (Instituto de Ciencias Sociales, 1969).   The files of Gallup Uruguay on the Tupamaro insurgency contain material on public perceptions of the Tupamaros and government policies, as well as political attitudes (e.g. support for revolutionary change).   Since the same questions are often repeated, it is possible to examine changes in public opinion and how it is affected by events.

Several excellent studies of Basque and Spanish public opinion were conducted in the post Franco period by Jimenez Blanco (1977), del Campo (1977), Esteban (1979), Linz (see Gordenker 1980), FOESSA (1989), Gunther, Sani and Shabad (1986). Clark (1984, 1990) presents data from a large number of surveys reported in the Spanish and Basque press.

For Northern Ireland, Rose, McAllister, and Mair (1978) presents polls on constitutional attitudes in Britain, the Irish Republic and Northern Ireland, during the 1968-78 period. The BBC (Northern Ireland) and the Irish Times carried out pre-election surveys in 1973,

1982 and 1985, and gave me copies of the detailed results. The Belfast Telegraph also provided me with copies of the polls they commissioned. *Fortnight Magazine* reports many surveys on Northern Irish politics, and such topics as internment. Moxon-Browne (1981), (1983) describes Catholic attitudes to the IRA, political prisoner status and constitutional aspirations.

International Gallup Polls, and *Index to International Public Opinion* contain several surveys on German and Italian attitudes to terrorism, anti-terrorist measures and revolutionary politics. The German polling organization, (Allensbach Institut fur Demoskopie), sent me all their surveys on terrorism. *L'Espresso,* (10 January 1982) reports the results of a survey on the Italian public's perceptions of the terrorists. A large number of Italian polls are reported in Fabris (1977) and Guidorossi (1984). The election studies by Penniman (1977, 1981) and Cerny (1978) also contain useful information.

Bibliography

Adams, J. (1986), *The Financing of Terror,* New English Library, London.

Alexander, Y. and Gleason, J. (eds) (1981), *Behavioral and Quantitative Perspectives on Terrorism,* Pergamon, New York.

Allen, R. (ed) (1969), *Violence and Riots in Urban America,* Jones, Worthington.

Althammer, W. (1978), *Gegen den Terror. Texte und Dokumente,* Bonn Aktuell, Stuttgart.

Altheide, D. L. (1987), 'Format and Symbols in TV Coverage of Terrorism in the United States and Great Britain', *International Studies Quarterly,* vol. 31, pp. 161-76.

Asociacion de Bancos del Uruguay, *Resumen de las principales aspectos de Actividad Economica del Uruguay,* Montevideo.

B.B.C. (1982), 'Attitudes to the Northern Ireland Assembly', *BBC Spotlight,* (October).

B.B.C. (1985), 'Opinion Poll', *BBC Spotlight,* (May).

Banco de la Republica Oriental del Uruguay, *Boletin Estadistico,* Montevideo.

Banfield, E. C. (1974), *The Unheavenly City Revisited,* Little Brown, Boston.

Becker, J. (1978), *Hitler's Children,* J. B. Lippincott, New York.

Bell, J. (1978), *A Time of Terror,* Basic Books, New York.

Boyle, K. (1980), *Ten Years On in Northern Ireland,* Cobden Trust, Nottingham.

Budge, I. and Farlie D. (1983), *Explaining and Predicting Elections, Issue Effects and Party Strategies in Twenty Three Democracies,* Allen and Unwin, London.

Burton, A. (1976), *Urban Terrorism: Theory Practice and Response,* Free Press, New York.

Cazzola F. (1974), *Local Politics, Development and Participation,* University Center for International Studies, Pittsburgh.

Cerny, K. H. (1978), *Germany at the Polls,* American Enterprise Institute, Washington.

Clark, M. and Irving, R. E. M. (1984), 'The Italian General Election of 1976', *Parliamentary Affairs,* vol. 30 (Winter 1977), pp. 8-31. University of Wisconsin Press,

Clark, M. and Irving R.E.M. (1972), 'Italian Political Crisis and the General Election of May 1972', *Parliamentary Affairs,* vol. 25 (Summer), pp. 198-223.

Clark, R. (1984), *The Basque Insurgents: ETA, 1952-80,* University of Wisconsin Press, Madison.

Clark, R. (1990), *Negotiating with ETA,* University of Nevada Press, Reno.

Clark, W. and O'Cinneide, B. (1981), *Tourism in the Republic of Ireland and Northern Ireland,* Cooperation North, Belfast.

Clutterbuck, R. (1978), *Kidnap and Ransom - The Response,* Faber, London.

Clutterbuck, R. (1973), *Protest and the Urban Guerilla,* Abelard Schuman, New York.

Corbetta, P. (1983), 'Perche piu indulgenza per i terroristi?', *Cattaneo,* vol. 3 (June).

Crenshaw, M. (1983), *Terrorism, Legitimacy and Power,* Wesleyan University Press.

Curtis, L. (1984), *Ireland: The Propaganda War,* Pluto Press, London.

Darby, J. and Williamson A. (1978), *Violence and the Social Services in Northern Ireland,* Heinemann,

Darby, John and Morris, G. (1974), *Intimidation in Housing, Northern Ireland Community Relations Commission,* Belfast.

Davis, R. and McGurnaghan P. (1975), 'Northern Ireland: The Economics of Adversity', *Quarterly Review of National Westminster Bank,* pp. 56-9.

Debray, R. (1967), *Revolution in the Revolution?,* Greenwood Press, Westport, CT.

Del Campo, S. (1982), *Terrorismo Internacional,* Instituto de Cuestiones Internacionales, Madrid.

Del Campo, S. (1977), *La cuestion regional espanola,* Editorial Cuadernos, Madrid.

Dynes, R. and Quarantelli, E. L. (1968), 'What Looting in Civil Disturbances Really Means', *Transaction,* (May) pp 9-14.

Equipo C. (1977), *Las Victimas del Post Franquismo,* Sedmay, Madrid.

Equipo D. (1984), *La Decada del Terror.* Ediciones Dyrsa, Madrid.

Esteban, J. (1979), *Las Elecciones Legislativas,* Centro de Investigaciones Sociologicas, Madrid.

Fabris, G. (1977), *Il comportamento politico degli italiani,* Franco Angeli, Milano.

Feierabend, I.K. and Feirabend, R.L. (1966), 'Aggressive Behaviors within Polities: A Cross-national Study', *Journal of Conflict Resolution,* pp. 244-341.

FOESSA. (1981), *Informe sociologico sobre el cambio politico en Espana 1975-81,* Madrid.

Galleni, M. (1981), *Rapporto sul Terrorismo,* Rizzoli, Milano.

Giner, J. (1983), 'Journalists, Mass Media and Public Opinion in Spain 1938-82, in Kenneth Maxwell (ed), *The Press and the Rebirth of Iberian Democracy,* Greenwood Press, Westport, CT.

Gordenker, Leon (ed) (1980), *Resolving Nationality Conflicts: The Role of Public Opinion Research,* Praeger, New York.

Gunther, R., Giacomo Sani, and Shabad G. (1986), *Spain after Franco,* University of California Press, Berkeley.

Gurr, T.R. (1968), 'A Causal Model of Civil Strife: A Comparative Analysis Using New Indices', *American Political Science Review,* pp. 162:1104-24.

Gurr, T. (1988), 'Empirical Research on Political Terrorism: The State of the Art and How It Might Be Improved', in R. W. Slater and M. Stohl (eds). *Current Perspectives on International Terrorism,* St. Martins, New York.

Hall, S. et al. (1978), *Policing the Crisis,* Macmillan, London.

Halperin, E. (1976), *Terrorism in Latin America,* Sage, Beverly Hills.

Hartman, H. (1970), 'Institutional Immobility and Attitudinal Change in West Germany', *Comparative Politics,* vol. 4 (July), pp. 579-92.

Heskin,K.   (1981),   'Social Disintegration in Northern Ireland', *Economic and Social Review,* (January) pp. 97-113.

Hewitt, C.   (1984),   *The Effectiveness of Anti-Terrorist Policies,* University Press of America, Lanham.

Hewitt, C.   (1990),   'Terrorism and Public Opinion: A Five Country Comparison',   *Terrorism and Political Violence,*   vol. 2 (Summer) pp. 145-70.

Hibbs, D.   (1973),   *Mass Political Violence: a Cross National Causal Analysis,* Wiley, New York.

Hirsch, J.   (1980, Der Sicherheitsstatt. Das Modell Deutschland, sein Krise und die neuen sozialen Bewegungen, Europaische Verlagsanstant.

Holland, J.   (1981),   *Too Long a Sacrifice,* Dodd, New York.

Irish Times. (1982), 'Public Reaction in N. Ireland to Aspects of the Prior Proposals', (May).

Irving, R.E.M. and Patterson, W. E. (1972), 'West German Election of November 1972', *Parliamentary Affairs,* vol. 26, (Winter) pp. 218-39.

Irving, R.E.M., and Paterson W.E. (1977), 'West German Election of 1976', *Parliamentary Affairs,* vol. 30, (Spring) pp. 209-25.

Irving, R.E.M., and Paterson W.E. (1981), 'West German Election of 1980', *Parliamentary Affairs,* vol. 34, (Winter) pp. 191-209.

Jenkins, B. (1975), *International Terrorism,* Rand, Santa Monica.

Jennings, A.   (ed)   (1988),   *Justice Under Fire,*   Pluto Press, London.

Jeschke, A. and Malanowski, W. (eds) (1980), *Der Minister und der Terrorist,* Rowohlt, Reinbek.

Kaase, M. and von Beyme, K. (eds) (1978), *Elections and Parties,* Sage, London.

Katz, R. (1980), *Days of Wrath,* Doubleday, New York.

Kaufman, E. (1979), *Uruguay in Transition,* New Brunswick, NJ.

Keesing's Contemporary Archives, (Weekly).

Knight, G. and Dean, T. (1982). 'Myth and the Structure of News', *Journal of Communication,* vol. 32 (Spring) pp. 162-71.

Kohl, J. and Litt, J.   (1974),   *Urban Guerrilla Warfare in Latin America,* MIT Press, Cambridge.

Kuper, L.   (1981),   *Genocide: Its Political Use in the Twentieth Century,* Yale University Press, New Haven.

Labrousse, A. (1979), *The Tupamaros,* Penguin, Harmondsworth.

Laqueur, W. (1977), *Terrorism,* Little Brown, Boston.

Lodge, J. (ed) (1981), *Terrorism: A Challenge to the State,* St. Martins Press, New York.

Lodge, J. (ed) (1988), *The Threat of Terrorism,* Westview Press, Boulder, Colorado.

Mack, A. (1981), 'The Utility of Terrorism', *Australian and New Zealand Journal of Criminology, vol. 14,* (December), pp. 197-224.

MacStiofain, S. (1975), *Revolutionary in Ireland,* Cremonesi, London.

Mayans, E. (ed) (1990), *Tupamaros,* Centro Intercultural de Documentation, Cuernavaca.

Meade, R. (1990), *Red Brigades,* St. Martins Press, New York.

McCann, E. (1974), *War and an Irish Town,* Penguin, Harmondsworth.

McGuire, M. (1973), *To Take Arms,* Macmillan, London.

Moss, R. (1972), *Urban Guerrillas,* Temple Smith, London.

Moss, R. (1973), *Chile's Marxist Experiment,* David and Charles, Newton Abbot.

Moxon-Browne, E. P. (1981), 'The Water and the Fish: Public Opinion and the Provisional IRA in Northern Ireland', *Terrorism,* vol. 5, pp. 41-72.

Moxon-Browne, E. P. (1986), 'Alienation: The Case of the Catholics in Northern Ireland', *The Journal of Political Science,* vol. XIV, (Spring).

Moxon-Brown, E. P. (1983), *Nation, Class and Creed in Northern Ireland,* Gower, Aldershot.

New Ireland Forum. (1983), *The Costs of Violence Arising from the Northern Ireland Crisis Since 1969,* Government Publications, Dublin.

O'Neill, B. (1980), *Insurgency in the Modern World,* Westview Press, Boulder, CO.

Paletz, D. L., Fozzard, P. A. and Ayanian, J. Z. (1983), 'The Terrorism on TV News: The IRA, The Faln, and The Red Brigades', in William C. Adams, (ed), *Television Coverage of International Affairs,* pp. 142-65, Ablex Publishers, Norwood, N.J.

Paletz, D. L., Fozzard, P. A. and Ayanian, J. Z. (1982), 'The I.R.A., the Red Brigades, the F.A.L.N. in the *New York Times',* *Journal of Communication,* vol. 32, (Spring) pp. 162-71.

Peeler, J. A. (1985), *Latin American Democracies,* University of North Carolina Press, Chapel Hill.

Penniman, H. (ed) (1977), *Italy at the Polls 1976,* American Enterprise Institute for Public Policy Research.

Penniman, H. (ed) (1981), *Italy at the Polls, 1979,* American Enterprise Institute, Washington, D.C.

Penniman, H. (ed) (1987), *Italy at the Polls 1983,* Duke University Press, Durham, NC.

Penniman, H. (ed) (1985), *Spain at the Polls,* Duke University Press, Durham, NC.

Pisano, V. (1979), *Contemporary Italian Terrorism: Analysis and Countermeasures,* Library of Congress, Washington, D.C.

Pitman, P. M. (1988), *Turkey: A Country Study,* Library of Congress, Washington, D.C.

Porzecanski, A. (1973), *Uruguay's Tupamaros,* Praeger, New York.

Raanen, U. et al. (1986), *Hydra of Carnage: The International Linkages of Terrorism,* Lexington Books, Lexington.

Rapoport, David (ed) (1988), *Inside Terrorist Organizations,* Columbia University Press, New York.

Rhoads, S. (ed) (1988), *Valuing Life: Public Policy Dilemmas,* Westview.

Rose, R. (1971), *Governing Without Consensus,* Beacon Press, Boston.

Rose, R., McAllister, I. and Mair, P. (1978), 'Is there a Concurring Majority about Northern Ireland', *Centre for the Study of Public Policy,* University of Strathclyde, Glasgow.

Rowthorn, B. (1981), 'Northern Ireland: An Economy in Crisis', *Cambridge Journal of Economics,* vol. 5 pp. 1-31.

Rude, G. (1964), *The Crowd in History: Popular Disturbances in France and England, 1730-1848,* Wiley, New York.

Rudolph, J. D. (1985), *Argentina: A Country Study,* Library of Congress, Washington, D. C.

Russell, C. (1974), 'The Urban Guerrilla in Latin America: A Select Bibliography', *Latin American Research Review,* vol. 9 (Spring), pp. 37-79.

Russell, C. et al. (1974), 'Urban Guerillas in Argentina: A Select Bibliography', *Latin American Research Review,* vol. 9, (Fall).

Russell, C. (1979), 'Statistics Italy 1978', *Terrorism: An International Journal,* vol. 2 .

Sanchez-Gijon, A. (1983), 'The Spanish Press in the Transition Period' in Robert P. Clark (ed), *Spain in the 1980's,* Ballinger.

Sani, G. (1975), L'immagine dei partiti nell'elettorato, in Caciagli, M. and Spreafico, A. (ed), *Un sistema politico alla prova,* il Mulino, Bologna.

Sani, G. (1975), 'Mass level response to Party Strategy', in Donald L. Blackmer and Sidney Tarrow (eds), *Communism in Italy and France,* Princeton University Press, N.J.

Sasson, D. (1981), *The Strategy of the Italian Communist Party,* Pinter, London.

Schmid, A. and de Graf, J. (1982), *Violence as Communication,* Sage, Beverly Hills.

Segaller, S. (1986), *Invisible Armies,* Michael Joseph, London.

Shapiro, S. (1972), 'Uruguay's Lost Paradise', *Current History,* vol. 62, pp. 98-103.

Silj, A. (1979), *Never Again Without a Rifle,* Karz, New York.

Sterling, C. (1981), *The Terror Network,* Holt, Rinehart and Winston, New York.

Stohl, M. (1988), *The Politics of Terrorism,* Marcel Dekker, New York.

Tarrow, S. (1989), *Democracy and Disorder,* Clarendon Press, Oxford.

Taylor, C. and Jodice, D. (ed) (1983), *World Handbook of Political and Social Indicators,* Yale University Press, New Haven.

Thompson, J. L. P. (1985), 'Crime, Social Control and Trends in Political Killing', Paper presented at the Annual Meeting of the Sociological Association of Ireland, Belfast.

Weinberg, L. and Eubank, W. *(1987),* The Rise and Fall of Italian Terrorism, Westview Press, Boulder, CO.

Uruguay: Poder Ideologia y Clases Sociales. Montevideo, 1970.

von Beyme, K. (1984), 'Do Parties Matter?', *Government and Opposition,* pp. 5-29.

von Beyme, K. (1985), *Policy and Politics in the Federal Republic of Germany,* St. Martins Press, New York.

Waddington, P. (1986), 'Mugging as a Moral Panic', *British Journal of Sociology,* vol. 38, (June).

Weinstein, M. (1975), *Uruguay: The Politics of Failure,* Greenwood Press, London.

Wilensky, H. L. (1975), *The Welfare State and Equality,* University of California Press, Berkeley.

Index